THE GOSPE
THE BRIEFC

by Ted DeMoss and
Robert Tamasy

CBMC
Publications
Chattanooga, Tennessee

The Christian Business Men's Committee is an international evangelical organization of Christian business and professional men whose primary purpose is to present Jesus Christ as Savior and Lord to other business and professional men and to train these men to carry out the Great Commission. (Matthew 28:18-20; Colossians 1:28-29)

CBMC of USA is a nondenominational, non-profit Christian organization supported by gifts from people committed to reaching and discipling business and professional men for Jesus Christ.

More information may be obtained by writing:
Christian Business Men's Committee of USA
1800 McCallie Avenue
Chattanooga, Tennessee 37404
615/698-4444

All Bible quotations are from the *New American Standard Bible* unless otherwise noted.

Fourth Printing, May 1987

Library of Congress Catalog Card Number 84-50535
ISBN 0-8423-1152-1, paper
Copyright © 1984 by Christian Business Men's Committee of USA
All rights reserved
Printed in the United States of America

CONTENTS

FOREWORD

Even before I finished Ted DeMoss' captivating new book, *The Gospel and the Briefcase*, I knew exactly where it fit in my library—right after the last chapter in the Book of Acts. Names have changed and two thousand years have passed, but the theme of the awesome power of the living God to transform men certainly hasn't.

This spiritual saga of the "Lord in the Marketplace" is a refreshing inner look at one of God's greatest movements, the Christian Business Men's Committee, and its godly and committed president, Ted DeMoss. In a day when Lifestyle Evangelism is finally back in vogue, CBMC stands head and shoulders above the masses as the leader that has been consistently practicing this method for more than half a century.

What an encouraging contrast is CBMC's style of evangelism to the now-popular "soft pew" mentality currently rampant in our churches. You will enjoy seeing how Ted doesn't wait for the average American to enter *our* hallowed church doors, but knocks at *their* office doors. Instead of fishing in our empty ponds, he casts his bait to the ocean surf. Uniquely presented, *The Gospel and the Briefcase* both illustrates and instructs at the same moment. In the midst of reading one of Ted's unforgettable stories, you will unexpectedly discover that you have just learned how better to witness. That is because Ted is a model of an evangelistic heart—so busy doing Christianity that your best bet to learn his secret is merely to follow in his footsteps.

Reminiscent of a well-known disciple, isn't it? One whose habit it was to go around his world visiting men in the marketplace. Once you realize that the ancient marketplace is now called the office park, you have the true biblical picture.

As your heart desires to beat a little more like Paul's, then this memorable classic may already have your name X'd on it.

Now turn the page and fall in stride with a modern-day disciple who "turns his world upside down" everywhere he goes. It begins with Acts 29, verse 1. . . .

Bruce H. Wilkinson
President, Walk Thru the Bible Ministries
Atlanta, Georgia

INTRODUCTION

In the United States today, there are an estimated 21 million business and professional men. Over the past thirty years, both as an insurance executive and since 1977 as president of the Christian Business Men's Committee of USA, I have had the opportunity to visit personally with thousands of these men. We have discussed mutual interests, problems, our outlooks on life. It is amazing how often our discussions seem to come back to the "bottom line," not only in terms of business but also in regard to what life is all about.

Each of the men I have met has been striving, as well as he knows how, to achieve a measure of happiness, fulfillment, a sense of meaning in his life. It is interesting to see the variety of ways in which the men seek to attain a degree of personal satisfaction.

The media offer us a number of suggestions. As we watch television commercials, read the billboards, and scan newspaper and magazine advertisements, we are told that success, fame, and admiration can be achieved in a multitude of ways. They can come as the result of using the right toothpaste and deodorant, or buying the right car, or taking vacations in the right places. Self-gratification, the ads tell us, can be accomplished by drinking the right liquor or beer, wearing the right aftershave, or having the right broker to handle our investments.

Movies, magazine and newspaper articles, and even our peers, give us other recommendations. The route to true happiness, society tells us, might be to dump our faithful wife of twenty years, trading her in for a newer, sleeker, flashier model. If pending parenthood seems inconvenient, there are ways of quickly resolving that problem. If business isn't going the way we would like, we can resort to "situation ethics" there, too. If all else fails, we can always abandon all our responsibilities, quit our job, move to a distant city, and start all over.

More often than I would like to remember, I have known businessmen and professionals—physicians, lawyers, engineers—who have opted for what they viewed as the "ultimate escape," a gun to the head and a squeeze of the trigger.

How does a person find happiness, inner peace, and the answer to "Why am I here?" Some feel that the solutions to those questions are more numerous than the blanks on a multiple-choice college exam. I don't believe that. I am convinced that there is only one true answer, and that He is the central figure of a book called the Bible. The sad fact is that the overwhelming majority of people across the United States have not even seriously considered Him as an alternative.

Of the 21 million business and professional men in our country, as well as we can determine, 19 million of them (90 percent) do not have a personal relationship with Jesus Christ. What makes that fact even more tragic is that many of them are unaware that such a relationship is even possible, since they have never heard a clear presentation of the claims of Christ.

It has been said that the saddest thing is not that men and women are lost, but rather that they do not know they are lost. Businessmen are no exception. In fact, perhaps more than any other segment of American society, business and professional men have been largely neglected by modern-day evangelistic efforts.

Many of our churches today, without question, are preaching the gospel of Jesus Christ. However, that message goes unheard by millions of unchurched businessmen. Even among those who are actively engaged in the church, many view their involvement as merely an "activity," one of the ways they build contacts to foster success in the marketplace. Often when the truth of Jesus Christ is presented in their churches, the message falls upon the unlistening ears of these men because their thoughts are dominated by such terms as "profit," "loss," "investment portfolio," "quarterly reports," and "the bottom line."

It is ironic that some of these men are church leaders, Sunday school teachers, respected members of their congregations. They may even have acquired a wealth of Bible knowledge, without ever having transferred the information in their heads to their hearts. Their religion just doesn't seem to relate to their personal lives or their businesses.

Herein lies the dilemma. The Bible tells us that "faith comes by hearing, and hearing by the Word of God." If businessmen are unchurched or in church but not "tuned in," how are they to be reached for Jesus Christ? More than fifty years ago, the Christian Business Men's Committee first recognized this problem and began, quietly but faithfully, to serve as a witness for Christ in America's marketplaces. In the decades since then, thousands upon thousands of business and professional men have heard fellow businessmen explain how their lives have been changed dramatically through the saving power of Jesus Christ. As a result, many men have been able to recognize their own spiritual need, and have turned their lives over to the Lord. These decisions have not only transformed the lives of individuals, but also have helped to bring about changes in the lives of their family members, as well as their work associates.

Even in the uppermost executive suites in our largest cities, God is using the ministry of the Christian Business Men's Committee—through its tandem purposes of evangelizing and discipling businessmen—to change lives. Through the unique outreach of CBMC, men at all levels of business—from the "movers and shakers" to men just starting out in their own small shops—are discovering that true joy is not found in earthly riches, but rather in eternal riches through Jesus Christ. For the first time, many of them are seeing that the only power on earth that really counts is the marvelous, transforming power of the Holy Spirit, helping them to find meaning and purpose in a world out of control. Proverbs 29:18 in *The Living Bible* states it clearly: "Where there is ignorance of God, crime runs wild. . . ."

In some evangelistic circles, the general attitude has been that "the businessman is unreachable" or that if he is to be reached, it will occur only if he should happen to stumble into a church and feel prompted to respond to an invitation. However, nearly every day, throughout CBMC, we hear stories which prove this simply is not true. The businessman can, and is, being reached for Jesus Christ. However, most often it is through another businessman, one who can relate to his personal needs, problems, and concerns.

It is not my intent in this book to promote an organization. Even though I am president of CBMC, I am committed primarily to the ministry to businessmen, not to the organization. If CBMC suddenly ceased to exist, it would not deter me from continuing what I have spent most of my adult years doing: sharing my faith in Jesus Christ with men in the business and professional world, praying that the Lord will continue to use me to challenge others who know Him to communicate that He is the one and only answer to life.

I thank God, however, for what the Christian Business Men's Committee of USA has meant in my life. It was through CBMC that I first learned of my God-given responsibility and then how to effectively communicate my faith to others. The Lord has used CBMC to equip many other men to do the same. For many years, despite nearly five hundred groups or "committees" of dedicated business and professional men, CBMC has been one of the best-kept evangelistic secrets. It is my hope that many of you who read this book will gain an understanding of our ministry and become motivated to take part in an outreach to unsaved businessmen.

This is not a history book, since our desire is not to dwell upon joys of the past, but rather to explain the "what," the "why," and the "how" of CBMC's ministry. In Christ's Great Commission, He commanded us to present the gospel to all nations and to every creature. We have focused on the business and professional men, knowing the important role they play in our society. The Lord Jesus Himself gave a substantial amount of his time to businessmen who ranged in status from the rich and powerful to poor fishermen who worked to provide for their daily existence. Over and over, the Book of Acts tells of leaders who were reached—such as the treasurer of Ethiopia, Barnabas, Saul, Cornelius, and Lydia.

It has been thrilling for me to see how the Lord has worked in the lives of men and their families over the years, bringing about changes that border on the miraculous. I cannot imagine a more challenging or fulfilling endeavor than to be used by God to help bring men to a saving knowledge of His Son. Best of all, it's something that each of us can do, if we are only willing to be available to Him, and to keep ourselves usable each day, so that our lives count for eternity.

Thank you for the opportunity to share with you CBMC's vision to spread the Good News of Jesus Christ throughout the marketplaces of the cities and towns of our great nation.

Ted DeMoss

CHAPTER ONE

THE IVORY TOWER

*Success is at best fleeting. The only way in which
a businessman can hope to achieve anything
remotely approaching lasting success is by striving
constantly for success in everything he attempts.*
J. Paul Getty

*But lay up for yourselves treasures in heaven,
where neither moth nor rust destroys, and where
thieves do not break in or steal.* Matthew 6:20

Expelling a sigh, William Tickle laid down his pen and leaned back in his chair. He pivoted to face the expansive window of his office in the Walnut Creek, California, corporate headquarters of Pacific Intermountain Express Co. Looking down on the parking lot below, he watched P-I-E clerical workers streaming toward their cars as another weekday came to a close. The raindrops pelting the windowpane seemed appropriate, since his mood was as dreary as the day. Bill hoped that, like the storm, his inner gloom would also pass quickly.

On his face was an expression which dimly reflected the confusion and turmoil which churned inside him. It was not his job which troubled him. He had been in the trucking industry for more than thirty years, and he couldn't imagine being involved in another line of work. The last seven years had been easier on his family, since he had settled into the post of executive vice-president for P-I-E in the San Francisco suburb. The frequent moves during the earlier years of his career had been difficult at times, uprooting the children from schools and severing friendships.

As he thought about Dorothy and his children, Bill realized that they were not the cause of his troubled frame of mind. Although they had experienced the normal conflicts of family life, there were no major problems. *Linda, Sandy, Debbie, and Mike have all been great kids,* he thought. His hard work and expertise had also been financially rewarding, enabling him to provide handsomely for all his family's needs.

True, the new federal legislation which was confronting the trucking industry was unsettling, but there wasn't much that he could do about that. Besides, he had dealt with more pressing problems in the past, and he was confident that he would help P-I-E to overcome any government-imposed setbacks.

Yet, that self-assurance was tempered somewhat by the knowledge that some of his associates and counterparts in other companies were not coping as well with the mounting pressures posed not only by new motor carrier laws, but also a struggling economy. In recent months, a number of men whom he knew well had suffered heart attacks or other illnesses which he felt were a result, if only indirectly, of the new stresses they were encountering.

What about me? Bill wondered. Physically, he felt fine, but he wondered if one day he would become a casualty of what by now was commonly being termed "executive stress." He also sensed that what was troubling him most was far deeper than concern for his physical well-being. An avid runner, Tickle kept his body in good shape; he had just been given a clean bill of health after an extensive physical checkup, so that was not cause for anxiety.

As he evaluated his life, he could only conclude that something was missing. But what? In frustration, he shook his head wearily as the rain continued to buffet the glass outside his comfortable office. *I have everything I've ever wanted. Still, it doesn't seem to be enough.*

Where is that sense of accomplishment, that feeling of fulfillment that I presumed came with the package? Hey, I'm a success. The company will get through this crisis a lot better than many of the others in the industry. *I'm living the American dream. Isn't that what they call the bottom line?*

Again he evaluated the separate elements of his life, keeping a mental checklist as he finished reviewing one area and moved on to the next.

Vague, perplexing questions began to form in his mind. *Is that all there is?* That Peggy Lee tune of years past suddenly seemed to take on a personal application. *After all those years of sweating, struggling, giving much of my life to this business, is that it? What do I do now? There must be more to life than this, isn't there?*

He struggled in vain to find satisfactory answers to his questions. After these many years, he knew the solution was not a promotion, a substantial pay raise, or even another job. The melodic buzz of his intercom snatched Bill out of his ruminations, and he quickly returned to work, setting aside his uneasiness—but only for the moment. The ongoing pressures of decision-making did not allow him much time for introspection; but in the days and weeks that followed, Tickle found himself confronted by those questions again and again, forcing him to initiate a personal search for some answers.

The executive suite. The apex of the American dream. Life, as society would have us to believe, is essentially an unending quest for the top. But, as Bill Tickle began asking, what happens when you have achieved your goals, when you have reached the highest rung of your career ladder? Looking at the question from another vantage point, what if one day you discover that you never will reach the pinnacle of achievement to which you have aspired? The Bible tells us that "many aspire, but few attain." Isn't that also true in the competitive world of business?

There is yet another category of businessmen: those who have weighed the costs inherent in the struggle to reach the top and have decided that they are unwilling to pay such a high price to ensure career advancement. Such men may have voluntarily lowered their job aspirations, but that does not necessarily provide them with satisfactory answers to the questions concerning the purpose and ultimate meaning of life. For them a new question may arise: "What IS 'worth it'?"

The story of Bill Tickle does not end with confusion and frustration. One day he found some answers to the perplexing questions of life, and it was largely due to the persistence and concern of a fellow businessman.

Soon after arriving at P-I-E in 1973, Tickle met Ken Beadle, who had recently retired as the safety director for P-I-E. Beadle had been the architect of the company's award-winning safety program, and his leadership was recognized throughout the industry.

It was more than Ken's expertise which impressed Bill, however; Beadle exhibited a sense of purpose which extended far beyond a continuing interest in the safety of P-I-E trucks, drivers, and cargo. He also showed a genuine interest and concern for Tickle.

One day Ken invited Bill to a Christian businessmen's luncheon in Oakland. Over the next few years, Tickle attended the noon meetings whenever he could, finding them to be enjoyable and relaxed, and perhaps even more important, not "religious." When a new committee was formed in Walnut Creek, Bill began attending the meetings there. "Ken kept after me to attend the breakfast meetings, and I went as often as possible. Speakers at the meetings frequently spoke about Jesus Christ; and although I wasn't too sure about what they had to say, I really liked the feel of the group," Bill says.

There was no pressure at the meetings for him to respond to the messages. The men at the meetings were much like himself, and Bill began to see that the terms "businessman" and "Christian" were not mutually exclusive. He began to rethink his own attitudes toward God. His parents had divorced when he was nine years old, and Bill's only childhood contact with church activities had been the occasional visit when he attended with a neighborhood friend.

After he and Dorothy had married in 1952 and had begun to raise a family, church participation seemed to be a natural thing, but Bill did not attach any special significance to it. He had always had a vague notion of the existence of God, and would pray on occasion during difficult times in his life. However, what he heard at the CBMC meetings—having assurance of eternal life and Jesus Christ having died so that men's sins might be forgiven—were all new ideas. Occasionally, he and Ken would discuss some of the points made during a luncheon talk, but for several years Bill resisted. "I wasn't sure that I was ready to accept that. I was afraid God would want me to do something I did not want to do, such as go to Africa or give up my career, our beautiful home, and our country club membership."

In 1980, Tickle went to a meeting where an executive from a California savings and loan company spoke. As he listened, Bill's clouded concept of God suddenly took on a clear focus. "It seemed as if the story the speaker told us that day about himself was a mirror of my life. He had no major problems, had a great family, and in general enjoyed a good life; but one day he realized that there had to be more to it than that. He then explained how he had committed his life to Jesus Christ, and what a difference that had made for him and his family."

That morning, Tickle said a simple prayer, asking Jesus Christ to come into his life. Looking back, Bill says, "I can wholeheartedly say that this was the most important decision I ever made." Since that day in July 1980, Bill Tickle has learned that there is indeed much more to life than attaining personal goals and acquiring many of the things that the world has to offer. He has discovered that there is no comparison to the peace and inner joy he experiences each day through Jesus Christ, regardless of what external circumstances he may have to face.

Across our country, there are millions of men like Bill Tickle, men who have reached the pinnacle of success in their fields. Unfortunately, most have not ventured beyond that point to realize that without a personal relationship with Jesus Christ, life will always be incomplete. Blaise Pascal has said, "The infinite abyss can only be filled by an infinite, immutable object . . . only by God Himself." Ignorant of this truth, men fall prey to disillusionment as they discover that the outward trappings of success and prosperity do not fulfill their hopes and expectations. To their dismay, they find that the famous words "Happily ever after" have been excluded from the job description. An often crushing realization is that such intangibles as "peace," "joy," and "satisfaction" do not come from outward successes, but rather from within.

In my travels around the country, I have met countless men who are devoting their entire lives to achieve what the world tells us will bring lasting happiness. We are constantly bombarded with messages such as, "You only go around once in life" and "Grab all the gusto you can." Men are endeavoring to find happiness in the latest model car, in clothes with the right designer labels, or in meals at the most exclusive restaurants. And yet, more times than I can remember, I have found that many prominent, successful businessmen are still asking the same question that Bill Tickle wanted to have answered: "Is that all there is?"

This challenging question brings about a variety of responses, some of them reflecting an inner feeling of despair. An article in the *Wall Street Journal*, for example, quoted a report on an American Medical Society study of suicides among its members in a five-state area. In many eyes, medicine is the most esteemed of professions; and yet the article reported, "The group wants to discover why the [suicide] rate for MDs, at one in 31 deaths, is twice the national average. . . ."[1]

An article in a different issue of the same newspaper told of another form of career tragedy: "After his promotion to an important management position in Europe, one executive just fell apart. . . . The executive started drinking heavily, which led to problems at home." A consultant quoted in the article said, "He dearly loves his wife, but they're separating fast. And now we have a casualty on our hands."[2]

Still another article in the *Wall Street Journal*, the so-called businessman's Bible, reports on the impact of stress upon a businessman and his family. "Stress is prevalent in business, especially small business."

"Hence, divorce is predominant among entrepreneurs," says a newsletter from the Center of Entrepreneurial Management, Worcester, Massachusetts.[3]

Articles in such respected publications as the *Harvard Business Journal*, *Industry Week*, and *Newsweek* echo such distressing accounts about businessmen. Our daily newspapers maintain an unofficial tabulation of this misery in the marketplace. The divorce rate is skyrocketing; drug abuse seems to have thoroughly infiltrated even the most affluent levels of society; there

---

[1] *Wall Street Journal*, 10 February 1981, p. 1, col. 5.
[2] Heywood Klein, "Fast Promotion Haunts Some in a Recession," *Wall Street Journal*, 19 March 1982, p. 29, col. 3.
[3] *Wall Street Journal*, 22 June 1981, p. 23, col. 1.

is an alarming increase of burnout among business and professional men, along with other symptoms of work-related stress. Perhaps saddest of all, suicides demonstrate a grim end to the perpetual question of "Is that all there is?"

Ours is a society that asks us to believe that the meaning of life can be found in self-gratification, self-realization, self-actualization—whatever you choose to call a self-oriented approach to life. Yet, over and over again, the statistics confirm for us that true fulfillment in life is not found in the people we know, what we do, or the things we have.

I am convinced that the questions regarding the meaning of life that business and professional men are asking in every part of our nation can be answered in one place: the Word of God. This book, compiled over thousands of years under the inspiration of the Holy Spirit, is God's enduring revelation to man. It is as relevant today for businessmen from Boston, Massachusetts, to Seattle, Washington, as it was centuries ago for merchants in ancient Jerusalem.

To everyone in our modern society desperately seeking to find direction and purpose, Jesus Christ stated, "I am the way, and the truth, and the life" (John 14:6). For those who have been striving in vain to achieve a richness, a fullness in life, Jesus made this promise: "I came that they might have life, and might have it abundantly" (John 10:10). As we look at the seeming futility, the uncertainty of our day-to-day existence, how are we to meet our needs or to cope with the inevitable problems which beset us? Jesus responded to this as well. He exhorted us to "seek first His kingdom . . . and all these things [our daily needs] shall be added to you" (Matthew 6:33).

I have seen, not only in my own life, but also in the lives of the countless men and women whom I have met from coast to coast and around the world, that

Jesus Christ is the singular answer to the troubles which continue to plague mankind. Everyone today wants an "abundant life," but there is widespread disagreement as to how such a life can be achieved. Jesus Himself said that an abundant life is possible, but only in His way, on His terms, both for now and after our time on earth has ended.

Communicating this truth to as many people as possible is the task to which I have committed my life. Our Lord has commanded us to be His witnesses, wherever we are in the world. Having spent many years of my life in business, I have become particularly burdened for the business and professional men of our nation, who make many of the key decisions which affect the operations of our towns and cities, and our nation.

The question is "How can men in the marketplace be reached for Christ?" Realistically, this can be done in a number of ways: through a local church service, a Christian television or radio program, a city-wide evangelistic crusade, or the reading of a book that clearly presents the gospel. But is there one "best" way of doing it, one approach that can offer maximum effectiveness?

I believe there is, and that is why I have given the illustration of how Bill Tickle came to know Jesus Christ as his personal Savior and Lord. Bill was reached primarily through a businessman, a man who was willing to unselfishly give of his life and his time to help guide another man to the truth.

When I was first introduced to the Christian Business Men's Committee of USA more than thirty years ago, it was this element that appealed to me—the commitment of a group of men to serve as representatives of Jesus Christ, systematically sharing the truths of the gospel with those they work with every day.

Even in the hundreds of fine, Bible-honoring churches where Jesus is preached as Savior and Lord, the typical businessman is not present, for the most part, to hear about the relevance of Jesus Christ in his everyday life. As for those millions of businessmen who attend church rarely or not at all, they may never hear God's message of grace in order to respond to it.

The Apostle Paul, in his letter to the church in Rome, makes clear the dilemma: "How then shall they call upon Him in whom they have not believed? And how shall they believe in Him whom they have not heard? And how shall they hear without a preacher? And how shall they preach unless they are sent? Just as it is written, 'How beautiful are the feet of those who bring glad tidings of good things!' " (Romans 10:14, 15).

For many of us, this passage immediately brings to mind the word *missionaries.* We think of missionaries in terms of foreign lands, such as Africa, Central and South America, Asia, and even Eastern and Western Europe. Yet an alien culture and a foreign language are not necessary criteria for establishing a mission. The need to see Jesus Christ demonstrated through the life of another person and then to hear the gospel clearly and simply communicated is just as great in a metropolis such as Houston, Texas, or Minneapolis/St. Paul, Minnesota, as it is in Sao Paulo, Brazil. As I see it, God's mandate for every Christian businessman is to serve as a "missionary in the marketplace."

Time after time, I have seen that if a businessman perceives a spiritual need, he is more likely to consult an associate he trusts, rather than a clergyman whom he does not know. It is a simple matter of confidence. When a businessman considers making an important investment, he will seek the counsel of a businessman he feels will offer some needed insight. If he needs financing, the businessman will turn to a peer whom he believes can help in that area. Even in recreational pursuits, businessmen are most likely to spend leisure time with other businessmen. It may seem strange to an outsider, but from a businessman's point of view, why should spiritual matters be treated any differently from other interests? The logical line of thinking for him is to seek out an individual who seems to have his life "all together" and then ask what is his secret, what are his answers to the fundamental questions of life.

There is, perhaps, no more effective way to communicate the impact of Jesus Christ upon your life than to practice what you preach; better yet, to practice it consistently before you even begin to preach. Over the years, I have found that the practical witness of a Christian businessman, as people observe his life day after day, is used by God in marvelous ways to bring others to an awareness of their need for Jesus Christ. Today, with the conflicting messages expressed by modern-day philosophers, the proliferating religious cults, and even apparently discordant views among churches, an individual is hard pressed to discern the truth. The businessman is particularly skeptical, since his judgments are relied upon for making so many critical decisions. All he is interested in is "What works?"

In business, there is no more persuasive element than the testimony of a "satisfied customer." As I see it, that should be the approach of the Christian businessman in sharing his personal faith with others—he is one such satisfied customer, and he is convinced that if others try it, they too will like it. Our challenge is to demonstrate that "what works" in our lives is Jesus Christ, who can have the same impact upon the lives of others, if they are only willing to let Him.

This, however, is no simple task. It takes time, commitment, dedication, and above all, faithfulness to the Lord. On our own, we are incapable of convincing even one person that the only way to achieve a truly fruitful, abundant life is through Jesus Christ. Yet, as the Holy Spirit works within us, and in the hearts of those we encounter each day, miracles can and do happen as lives are turned around by the saving power of the Lord Jesus.

In the pages to come, I will be telling you more about the ministry of businessmen to businessmen, introducing you to the tremendous stories of some of the men I have met whose lives have been transformed through Christ. I will also explain some of the approaches which we have found to be most effective in the mission of evangelizing and discipling business and professional men.

First, I would like to tell you about the turning point in my own life.

CHAPTER TWO

REACHING OUT

We know the truth, not only by the reason, but by the heart. Blaise Pascal

And you shall know the truth, and the truth shall make you free. John 8:32

I'm one of those fellows who became a Christian several years after joining a church. (Our Greek surname, Demosthenes, was shortened and Americanized to DeMoss.) My parents were good, hard-working Greek immigrants. My father did not go to church the first forty-five years of my life, yet he was a very fine man. My mother attended church only occasionally, perhaps on Christmas or Easter.

I was convinced that there was a God, a heaven, and a hell. My father never mentioned them, but I was convinced they existed. One question bothered me more than anything else in the world: "Who goes where?" I also wanted to know how God decides who goes where; I figured it was His decision, not mine. I came to the conclusion that if you're good you go to heaven, and if you're bad you go to hell. So I tried to live a good life; I really made an effort to walk the way I thought God would want me to walk. As a young man I even started attending Sunday school and church, which was strange since my parents didn't go.

I didn't know one church from another, so I picked a big name-brand church and attended it for a number of years. I eventually joined the church and had water put on my head; I got my own box of envelopes, but I still didn't know one thing about whether I would go to heaven or hell. I didn't know if I had done enough good things for God to accept me, so I was constantly troubled that I might fall short of whatever He would require.

Several years later, after I had joined the church and even received a certificate saying that I was an official member of one of the largest denominations in America, I was taken to a meeting where a man explained that it is not good people who go to heaven and bad people who go to hell—simply because there *aren't* any good people. He pointed out that every man and woman alive has broken every one of the Ten Commandments, in thought, word, or deed.

That night, the fellow explained to me something I had never heard before. He said that there is one thing that separates people from God, and that is sin. We've all sinned; we've all missed the mark. He then pointed out that the Bible said God made Jesus Christ to be sin for us; and since Christ had no sin of His own, we can have the righteousness of God through Jesus Christ. As teenagers might state it today, Christ took the rap for us. That night, by faith, I accepted God's provision for my sin through Jesus Christ.

That night I lost my religion and began a relationship. I came to realize that religion and Christianity are entirely different. Religion, according to the dictionary, is man's best effort to find God. Christianity is the opposite: God's best effort to find man. You spell *religion* with two letters: "Do!" Christianity is spelled with four letters: "Done." That is what Christ meant when he hung on the cross and said, "It is finished."

On that night, I began a new life with purpose, direction, and values that I could never fully explain. For the first time, I understood that although I was not a perfect man, I was a *forgiven* man in God's sight. That night I also received some fantastic advice, namely that I should read the Bible every day. I've been doing that now for more than forty years. I don't know how many times I have read the Bible cover to cover. In the beginning it was extremely important because I was getting little outside spiritual food.

I did not learn a great deal studying the Bible on my own, but I did find out a few things. One of the most important discoveries I made was that, as a Christian, I had to marry a Christian. It seemed clear to me from the Scriptures that I could not expect God to bless my home if I didn't marry a believer. While in pre-flight training at the University of North Carolina, I met Edith. On our first real date together, we went to church. A couple of years after the war ended, we got married (while I still had one year to go in college) on August 30, 1947. On our wedding night, we started reading the Bible and praying together. However, we had almost no involvement with any church in those days.

In early 1951, something very important happened in my life. The previous year my cousin and close friend, Art DeMoss, had committed his life to Christ. Art, who passed away in 1979, was only forty days older than I. In 1951, he took me to a Christian Business Men's Committee prayer meeting. A new group had been formed in Albany, New York, and he was a charter member. I had never heard of CBMC. There were only four men who attended besides me—Art and three others—but all four had hearts for God. It was on a Thursday night, and I met with these men for one hour as they prayed for other men—by name. They must have prayed for several hundred men. In my hometown, you could have prayed for almost anyone: I knew so few Christians.

My first reaction was that these had to be the craziest guys I had ever known. They were praying for all those people and planning to invite many of them to a dinner at our finest hotel where a businessman would tell how he met Jesus Christ. To top it off, they weren't asking each member to bring one unsaved man. That would mean only eight men total, and if I came it would be nine. Instead, they were each committed to bringing ten unsaved men to their first outreach meeting, and they were asking God to have forty-five men there that night: the four members, the forty unsaved guests, and the speaker. (I messed up their numbers when I showed up— without a guest!)

To be honest, I went but I didn't have any confidence in the affair. It seemed kind of flimsy to me for four men to pray for forty lost men to attend a religious meeting. Actually, they had been faithfully praying for the meeting over a series of weeks, but that still didn't convince me.

The night of the meeting, a businessman spoke, presenting his simple testimony of how he had received Christ. I saw several men give their lives to Christ before they left the dining room. I could hardly believe it! I had been a Christian for several years; but now, at the age of twenty-five, for the first time I saw someone converted. I had thought this was what the church is supposed to do; but these men showed me that if I started to pray for men who did not know Jesus Christ, and then shared the Good News in any one of several ways, I could see some of my friends come to Christ.

Before long I became a member of CBMC, and I started to pray that before I died, the Lord would let me see just one person commit his life to Christ as a result of my ministry and testimony. To help me, the CBMC men told me that to be used by God to win a man to Christ, there are a few basic requirements. First, you can have no known sin in your life. Next, you have to pray. They pointed out that it is a waste of time to pray, "God use me," simply because it is not scriptural. Rather, we should pray, "God keep me usable." He uses people who are usable. I also learned that you don't even have to pray for ability, since ability has nothing to do with winning people to Christ. It's availability; you just have to be available to be used by God.

They also showed me a few other "basics." For example, they demonstrated how you can take the third chapter of the Gospel of John, using the first eighteen verses to let God's Word tell the story. Back then we did not have booklets such as the one we use today in CBMC, *Steps to Peace with God.* Next, they told me to pray every day that God would keep me sensitive to the needs of those around me and that He would show me when I'm supposed to speak to someone. That, they explained, is the work of the Holy Spirit.

I began praying in this way. In my job of selling insurance, I walked into an apartment building to call on a man whose name had been sent to our office on a card. Responding to a direct mail lead, I went to the door of a third-floor apartment. The man inside spoke through the door without opening it and asked, "Who's out there?"

Part of our training in selling insurance was that you never say, "the insurance man," because people won't open the door. So I just said, "I'm Ted DeMoss."

He said, "I don't think I know you," and I responded, "No, you don't."

The man inside began to get defensive: "If I open this door, I'll knock you down those stairs. Get away from my door." Since I sincerely thought that he needed insurance, I replied, "Mister, I'm not going to hurt you. Please open the door. I've got to talk to you."

I fully intended to talk with the man about insurance, since from the referral card it appeared that he might be interested. But when he opened the door, I saw that there was no point in that. I saw a man with a white beard who looked like Santa Claus, except he was very thin. I hadn't been in the business that long, but I knew he was too old for insurance. I learned later that he was eighty-one years old.

He looked directly at me and said, "I opened the door. Now, what do you want to talk about?"

"I want to come in and talk to you."

"What do you want to talk about?" he asked.

"May I come in?" I persisted. Even as I said this, I felt impressed by the Spirit of God to talk with this man, a complete stranger, about Jesus Christ. I had never done that before in my life.

Finally, he said, "Come in, then." I entered, and we both sat down on the couch in the living room. Looking me straight in the eye, the elderly man said, "Go on, tell me what you want to talk about."

I paused just for a moment, and then said the only thing that came to my mind: "I want to read the Bible to you." Talk about no training in witnessing for Christ! I had absolutely no preparation, aside from what my CBMC friends had told me about using the third chapter of John.

"Go ahead," he said.

"I don't have a Bible," I told the man. "Do you have a Bible?"

I didn't know what was going through his mind at that point, but he answered, "I don't know whether I have a Bible or not. I'm blind." I had not even noticed the man was blind!

Having arrived prepared to sell insurance, not to tell someone about Jesus Christ, I asked the man if I could look around the apartment for a Bible. He told me that was all right. Quickly, I said a silent prayer: "Lord, help me to find a Bible," and then I added, "and don't let me leave home again without a Bible, a New Testament, or something." After a brief search, I did find a Bible, covered with dust on top of a stack of books.

I walked back to the couch and did just what the CBMCers told me. I opened up the Bible to the third chapter of John and slowly read the first eighteen verses to my new friend sitting beside me. I never looked at him as I read. In fact, the further I read, the more scared I got because I couldn't remember what I should do next. The fact is, the CBMCers had never told me what to do next. So I just read, slower and slower, until I got to verse 18, "He who believes in Him is not judged; he who does not believe has been judged already, because he has not believed in the name of the only begotten Son of God."

As I finished that last verse, I prayed for the Lord to give me wisdom as to what I should do. I looked over at the old man, and what I saw shocked me—his beard was wet with tears because of what had just been read to him from the Bible. I wasn't trained, but I still had enough sense to realize that God had indeed spoken to this man through His Word.

"Sir, would you like to invite Jesus Christ into your life now, right here?" The man said, "Well, I would like to do it right now, but not right here."

"Where do you want to go?" I asked him.

He answered, "I want to do it with my mother." Mentally, I was scratching my head. The man had told me he was eighty-one years old, and I thought, *What do I say now?*

I decided to ask, "Where is your mother?"

"In the kitchen," he replied.

Well, I supposed there probably was a picture of her in the kitchen, and he wanted to go in there for sentimental reasons. We made our way back to the kitchen, and to my surprise, there was his mother. She was ninety-eight years old and an invalid, sitting in a canvas-backed chair. I can hear the man's words as if he were speaking them today: "Mother, God has sent a man to our home."

I had gone on this call thinking the insurance company had sent me, but I realized that what he was saying was true. Then he said, "He's been reading the Bible to me, and I'm going to accept Jesus Christ." I don't believe I have ever heard a woman scream like she did in my life! They probably heard her all the way down on the first floor. When she regained control of her emotions, the aged woman said an amazing thing: "Mister, I don't know who you are, but I have prayed for my boy every day for over eighty years. I knew Jesus Christ as my personal Savior when my son was born, and I've prayed for him all these years."

Her son, eighty-one years old and blind, and I got on our knees, and I had the joy of praying with him and seeing him come to Jesus Christ. God had answered two prayers: hers of eighty years and mine of just a few weeks.

In the Bible, I had read that "some plant, some water, and God gives the increase." I had been there to partici- pate in the increase, but I hadn't done any planting or any watering. The man's faithful mother had done most of it. I also learned, however, that a Christian man on the first floor of the building had been taking care of their physical needs for several years. Neither of them was able to leave the house, so the man would come up every day and get their grocery order, find out what other needs they had, and take care of them.

The first year that the downstairs tenant worked with the old woman and her son, he would bring his Bible to their apartment and read from it until the son told him to stop. When I left that morning, the blind man asked me to go by their friend's apartment and ask him to start bringing his Bible with him again.

I was so excited that I didn't work the rest of the day. Edith was working as a registered nurse at the hospital, on the 11 P.M. to 7 A.M. shift. I drove home and woke her up. I don't know if she appreciated that, but I had to tell her what had happened. God had answered the simple prayer of a fellow who really didn't know much and had

given me the joy of helping a person to find Christ. I
went back to visit him one time before I moved to
Chattanooga, Tennessee, later in the year. It is
amazing—when I try to think of other events that happened in 1951, I can't remember anything more
significant than this experience!

That is how I got started with the Christian Business
Men's Committee. I was twenty-five years old. I feel
strongly that the only way you can justify involvement
in anything is because it works. Every day, all across
our country, men are sharing the story of Jesus Christ
with other businessmen because, as was true in my life,
a layman first challenged me to do it. That is exactly
what the Apostle Paul said to his disciple Timothy, to
teach "faithful men, who will be able to teach others
also" (2 Timothy 2:2).

That does not mean that a businessman has to quit
his job to spend time addressing men's spiritual needs.
In fact, the opposite is true. Men can effectively serve
God right where they work. There is no greater testimony than that of a man who has taken a stand for
Jesus Christ and who also demonstrates a commitment
to excellence in business. I have had men tell me they
didn't think a person could be a businessman and a
Christian. I could not disagree more. In fact, with the
many pressures facing the businessman in today's fast-
paced, rapidly changing society, I can't see how he can
cope from day to day *without* being a Christian. Jesus
Christ not only offers each of us the hope of eternal life,
but also promises a supernatural source of help, wisdom, and strength for everyday living.

There are millions of businessmen in America today
who are looking for answers. And there are many
Christian businessmen across the nation who would
like to help them; unfortunately, many reluctantly
admit, "I don't know how."

Beginning in the next chapter, we will look at the "how-to" of reaching the business and professional man for Jesus Christ.

CHAPTER THREE

HOW ABOUT LUNCH?

I have but one lamp by which my feet are guided, and that is the lamp of experience. I know no way of judging the future but by the past.
Patrick Henry

Again therefore Jesus spoke to them, saying, "I am the light of the world; he who follows Me shall not walk in the darkness, but shall have the light of life." John 8:12

For years, we have found that one of the best ways to present the truths of the gospel to business and professional men is during a mealtime outreach meeting. These meetings, held at breakfast, lunch, or dinner, are conducted much like secular functions, with one exception: the speaker, always a business-man, relates the experiences in his own life that led to his personal commitment to Jesus Christ.

Since I first became involved with the Christian Business Men's Committee, I have been privileged to speak to groups of men (or men and their wives) on countless occasions. It never ceases to amaze me how the Lord can work through the simple testimony of a business-man to touch the minds and hearts of other men.

These meetings have frequently been referred to as "mealtime evangelism," but in reality they are much more than that. One of our members, years ago, explained it this way: "What we do at an outreach meeting is very similar to one beggar telling another beggar where he can find some bread."

No one on this side of eternity will ever fully be able to measure the results of what has taken place at outreach luncheons and dinners across America. For more than three decades, I have seen thousands and thousands of men indicate that they have accepted Jesus Christ as Savior for the first time. We realize that, for many men, such an indication might be their way of "crying out for help" as they begin to sense their own spiritual need. (In chapter five, which deals with following up on men who express such concern, we will discuss this aspect in some detail.) However, I can recall many instances which illustrate in a dramatic way what can, and often does, happen when unsaved men attend outreach functions.

One that stands out vividly occurred several years ago when I was invited to speak at a Christmas couples' CBMC banquet in Dalton, Georgia, just thirty miles from Chattanooga. Before I agreed to be the speaker, I made one stipulation. I said that I would be willing to go, provided that at least half of those in the audience would be non-Christians. At the time I was in the insurance business full time, so I suggested to the chairman of the Dalton committee that he should have each member bring his life insurance salesman, the man who handles his homeowner's insurance, the fellow who sold him his automobile policy, or any other insurance man he might know.

The committee agreed that there would be at least a 50:50 ratio of non-Christians to Christians at the dinner. I drove to the Holiday Inn in Dalton with my wife on Monday evening, December 10; and true to their word, the men had seen to it that there were more unsaved men and women there than Christians.

During my talk I explained how I had reached the point of deciding to receive Jesus Christ as my personal Savior and Lord, then told of how Christ had changed my life and the lives of some people I knew. At the close, I suggested that those who wanted to commit their lives to Christ could follow me in repeating silently to themselves a brief prayer that I said aloud.

After I dismissed the meeting, a man in his mid- to late thirties came up to me and started asking questions faster than I could answer them. I was trying to respond to each of his questions as carefully as possible; but then he looked over his shoulder and saw a number of other men who were waiting to speak with me. "Well, it looks like there are a lot of other people who want to talk to you. I shouldn't bother you," he said. I tried to encourage him to stay, but he said good-bye and left.

Thirty or forty minutes later, the same man came back into the banquet room just as Edith and I were preparing to leave. He said that he and his wife had started to drive home, but halfway there he told her that he felt he needed to go back and talk to me further. His wife, for reasons unknown to me, refused to come into the room, choosing instead to wait outside in their car. Nevertheless, the man, whom I discovered was a district manager for a well-known insurance company, sat down with me and for thirty minutes asked questions about the person of Jesus Christ—the purpose of His life as well as the purpose of His death, and several other matters.

When his questions were finally exhausted and our conversation seemed to be coming to a close, I asked him if he would like to commit his life to the One who had made him. The man declared that it was his desire to do this, so we bowed our heads and he prayed to accept Christ as his Savior.

Then he had another question: "What do I do next?" I told him that the first thing he should do is to take his wife and children to Sunday school and church the very next Sunday. He admitted that he had no idea what church he should go to, or where he could find one in which he would feel comfortable. I suggested one that I knew was sound and true to the gospel. We even looked up the address in the telephone book. The insurance man promised that he would go.

Next, I told him that I would like him to be at the CBMC prayer breakfast the following Monday morning. The group met weekly for prayer and Bible study, and I felt that he would benefit from attending. However, when I told him the breakfast was at 6:30 A.M., he said he couldn't possibly be up that early. I then said that I would make him a deal: If he would get up and attend, I would drive the thirty miles from Chattanooga and be there so that I could introduce him to the CBMCers.

"You would come all that way just to get me there?" I assured him that I would; and once he was convinced, we agreed that we would meet the following Monday morning, December 17.

As he had promised, he arrived on time. He told me he *was* in church the day before, Sunday, with his family. The insurance executive enjoyed the breakfast so much that he commented that he would like to join CBMC. One of the men gave him an application blank, which he said he would bring back the following Monday with his check.

The new Christian never made it back to the breakfast. Two days later, on December 19, he came home from work around 4:00 P.M. Due to his responsibilities in overseeing all the agents working for his company in northern Georgia, he rarely left the office that early. However, on that particular afternoon he told his wife he was feeling very tired and was going to take a nap before supper. When his wife went to awaken him at 5:30, he was dead.

Imagine: Just nine days before stepping into eternity, he had met the Savior who became Lord of his life. The only time he had ever been in church was that Sunday between December 10 and 19. Aware of what had transpired in her husband's life during that brief period, his wife called me to ask if I would be willing to conduct his funeral. (She had gotten my name from one of the

Dalton CBMCers.) Since I was a businessman and had never done anything like that, I suggested she contact the pastor of the church they had visited and request that he handle the service. He graciously agreed to do it.

As I reflect upon this story, it strikes me that it could have been quite different. What if the CBMC member who had purchased insurance from the man had not invited him to the banquet? What if that CBMCer, rather than thinking about the spiritual welfare of his insurance man, had just attended on his own to hear another testimony? Or what if he had concluded, "That's just too much money to spend for dinner, let alone to pay for another couple too"? Fortunately, those questions never had to be addressed, and I know that heaven rejoiced over the faithfulness of a concerned Christian businessman.

We have found that mealtime outreach meetings have been an extremely effective means for presenting the gospel to non-Christians in a low-key, unpressured setting. By intent, the meetings are tailored with the lost businessman, rather than the Christian, in mind. There are no Bibles on the tables, no singing of hymns, no pro-longed prayers other than a simple return of thanks for the meal. We purposely avoid table talk which relates to spiritual matters. We leave ashtrays on the tables for those who might want to use them.

Our desire is for our uncommitted guests to be com-fortable at our meetings, to experience the friendship of Christian men, and to remain open and receptive to the speaker's message. We are fully aware that it is the Lord, not any powers of persuasion, that brings the increase; and yet we do not want to erect any barriers to the working of the Holy Spirit when the speaker tells about his relationship with Jesus Christ. At the close of his talk, guests may not yet be ready to give their hearts to Christ, but at least they will have heard something to think about.

I think of another instance in which a man approached me after a meeting in a midwestern city. Like the insurance manager, he began firing one question after another. He told me that in all his life, he had never heard a story like the one I had just told. Apparently he had had little or no contact with a church, and had never heard anything about God's provision for his sins.

As other men began pressing in around us, apparently wanting to talk to me, this man also became discouraged and started to walk away in despair. As he was stepping away, I asked him for his business card; when I got home I wrote him a lengthy letter trying to explain the gospel in more detail. I also sent him a small book we use extensively in CBMC, *The Reason Why,* which was written by a New Zealand CBMCer to his employees to explain his Christian faith.

Six months later, the man from the midwestern city wrote to tell me that because of the letter I had mailed to him and the impact of one or two other Christian businessmen in his life, he had become a brand-new person in Jesus Christ. I later discovered that this fellow had been featured in local newspapers as one of his city's "Ten Most Eligible Bachelors." Yet, at the age of thirty-nine, he had known absolutely nothing about the Lamb of God who could take away his sin, as well as the sin of the world.

Soon afterward he joined CBMC and became an active member, even taking part in starting a new committee in his area. Three years later, still a young man at forty-two, he suffered a massive heart attack and God took him home. Again, this was a case of a man hearing a presentation of the gospel for the first time at a CBMC mealtime outreach meeting.

Although I have spoken at such functions more times than I can remember, I take no pride in it. In fact, it is humbling to realize that while the Lord could have chosen an infinite number of ways to accomplish his purpose, He decided to work through men and women to win others to Himself. An outreach speaker is nothing more than an instrument of God, a man who is usable and available so that the Lord can speak through him. It has been my joy over the years to meet many men who have been reached for Christ through this ministry of one businessman to another. In the final analysis, it is very assuring to know that it is God's job alone to keep track of the souls being harvested.

One day I was at work in Chattanooga when I received a telephone call from a man who identified himself as "someone I had met" four years ago. Being very busy that day, I tried to decline his invitation to have lunch with him. I finally agreed to go when he stated, "You're the one who introduced me to Jesus Christ, and I want to tell you about it."

We met at a restaurant downtown. He lived in Tulsa, Oklahoma, and was in town on business. He was somewhat shocked that I did not remember him. I had to admit that not only did I not remember him, but I also did not recall the events that he said took place the night we met.

He told me he had attended his first CBMC meeting in Tulsa where I was the speaker. He said his response to hearing my testimony was to become extremely upset. In fact, when I finished speaking, he said that he walked up to me and shook his finger in my face, condemning everything that I had said and that I stood for. Although the incident had escaped my memory, he told me that he had gone to great lengths to try to get me upset or to argue with him, but I wouldn't. He had even told me what church he belonged to and how faithfully he had worked in that church. He asserted that there certainly could be no way that God would not accept him, in light of all that he had done for the church.

At the end of this essentially one-sided conversation, he said I had asked for his business card. Soon after I had returned to Chattanooga, he said I had sent him a letter, along with a copy of *The Reason Why*. It was through the reading of that little booklet that he had given his heart to Jesus Christ.

After recounting what had happened at the meeting years before, the businessman told me that he had become affiliated with an excellent evangelical church in Tulsa, had joined CBMC, and had kept the letter I mailed him under the glass on his desk as a constant reminder of how lost he had been. The letter, he said, also helped to keep him mindful that most of the people who come into his office to do business are equally lost.

In fact, the letter had become a sort of conversation piece, the businessman noted, since people frequently ask him about it. As a result, the letter would serve as a focal point for redirecting the conversation to what Jesus Christ had done for him. On a subsequent visit to Tulsa, I had an opportunity to visit him in his office. That letter was still under the glass on his desk to remind him of his own "before" and "after."

The Christian Business Men's Committee traces its beginnings back to 1930, when a small group of Christian businessmen in Chicago planned a series of large-scale, noon-hour meetings to offer hope to the people of that city in response to the growing despair of the Great Depression. During those daily meetings, thousands of people heard businessmen give clear presentations of the claims of Jesus Christ, and many responded by turning their lives over to the Lord.

Simultaneously, similar groups were established in other parts of the country, and they continued to address deeply rooted spiritual needs for the duration of the Depression. As the nation's economy rebounded, the groups consolidated. From the 1940s until 1973, the organization was known as Christian Business Men's Committee International. Activities ranged from evangelistic street meetings, city-wide evangelism crusades, evangelistic centers for servicemen, to radio programs, men's fellowship meetings, jail services, conferences, and other endeavors aimed at helping people to find their way to Christ.

In the early 1960s, however, CBMC began to narrow its focus, and gradually its purpose became redefined to what it is today: "To present Jesus Christ as Lord and Savior to business and professional men, and to develop Christian business and professional men to carry out the Great Commission." This stated purpose helped CBMC, in business terminology, to "define its market," recognizing the value of directing efforts toward a clearly specified target. Those men in CBMC understood that every man, woman, and child has an equal need to know the Lord Jesus Christ personally; but they also realized that the American businessman is the one segment of society not being approached directly by any other evangelistic organization.

With this new focus, the mealtime outreach meeting became a key element in the CBMC ministry. It remains the same today. Often men, who for whatever reason will not set foot inside a church, agree to be guests at a CBMC luncheon or dinner. Some respond to the conviction of the Holy Spirit the first time they attend. Others make repeat visits before surrendering their hearts to Christ. Still others (similar to Bill Tickle whom you met in an earlier chapter) attend dozens of times, stopping short of making a commitment, but they keep returning because they sense "something different" about the men they meet.

But what is the power behind these monthly meetings? What is it that prompts these non-Christian men to attend a function which is clearly "Christian"? And how is it that these men not only attend, but also arrive ready to hear a discussion of spiritual matters, many times even receptive enough to make a personal decision for Christ?

The answer to each of these questions is *prayer.* In the next chapter, we will take a look at the vital role that prayer plays in the ministry of businessmen to other businessmen.

CHAPTER FOUR

TALKING TO GOD ABOUT MEN

I shall never believe that God plays dice with the world. Albert Einstein

At all times [men] ought to pray and not to lose heart. Luke 18:1

I f I were to pinpoint the one key element in determining the effectiveness of the ministry to businessmen (or the success of any Christian endeavor, for that matter), I would have to say that it is prayer. E. M. Bounds, in his great book on prayer, wrote, "How dare we ever talk to men about God, until we have first talked to God about men." I believe that a missing ingredient in the lives of most Christians who are trying to witness to others has been well verbalized in that simple statement.

As I have traveled around the country, I have observed that the hub of each fruitful Christian Business Men's Committee has been the weekly prayer breakfast portion of our ministry. Once a week, in addition to Bible study and fellowship, the men spend approximately thirty minutes praying for men they know, by name, asking the Lord to convict those individuals of their need to give their hearts to Jesus Christ. That may sound easy enough, but over the years I have learned that you can get people to do almost anything—except to pray.

To be honest, it doesn't even sound exciting to get

up at 5:30 in the morning to meet with other Christian men at 6:30 to pray for half an hour for men who do not know Jesus Christ. It can become somewhat discouraging, and sometimes even monotonous, because God works in his own time, and results often seem slow in coming. If a man is faithful in attending the prayer breakfasts, he may go for months praying for many of the same names again and again. From our perspective, it may appear as if nothing is really happening. I have to admit that I sometimes get to a point where I wonder what it is going to take to reach a certain individual for Christ. Often, at such times, the Lord will have someone remind me that "the fervent prayer of a righteous man availeth much" and that if we pray, God can and will work.

In addition to my involvement in CBMC meetings, my wife, Edith, and I have used our home for outreach purposes for many years. We have had as many as thirty or thirty-five couples come over for the purpose of sharing with them what God has done in our lives. Together we have visited every home on our street at one time or another, inviting the people over for dinner. Many times we have relearned the lesson of being consistent and faithful in our prayers for lost friends and neighbors. We have seen many of our prayers answered, even if not in the ways we expected.

On one occasion I invited some neighbors—a man, his wife, and two sons—to our house for dinner. They agreed to come on a Friday night. In fact, the man asked if we could eat at 5:30, since he did not sleep well if he ate a late meal. We told them that would be fine, and on Friday night we had the dinner ready for my wife, our three daughters, plus this neighborhood family of four. At quarter to six, they still had not arrived. Because he lived just a couple of doors away, I walked over to his home and rang the doorbell. He came to the door barefoot in his undershorts. It seemed obvious to me that he had forgotten his dinner appointment with us.

When I reminded him that this was the night that he was supposed to come over, he casually replied, "Oh, we're not coming." When I indicated my amazement, he said, "I heard that you are religious people, and we don't want to get involved with you." I could hardly believe what he was saying! The man admitted that he had not taken the time to call us, but even at that he did not offer an apology. I told him that the food was ready, and I even tried to encourage him to come late; but he just said for us to eat twice as much that night. He firmly insisted that he was not coming.

During the next eight years I made repeated efforts to become his friend, but with no success. I invited him on many occasions to attend a CBMC luncheon meeting, but he never accepted. In fact, I could not even talk to him directly over the telephone. All I could do was to leave messages. I did the only other thing that was left: I (and other CBMCers) continued to pray for his salvation.

More than eight years after that first dinner invitation, a bald-headed man walked into one of our luncheons, and at the close of the meeting, was converted to Jesus Christ. This man was not my neighbor; in fact, I did not know him at all. The only reason he caught my attention was because of his unusual appearance. He was dressed neatly, but he had as much hair on his head as you would find on a marble-topped table. That kind of man sticks out in a crowd.

A month passed and it was time for our next CBMC luncheon. As the Lord would have it, it was my turn to speak. The bald-headed man also came to this meeting, but this time he brought with him my neighbor, for whom we had been praying for so many years. When my neighbor saw me, and particularly when he discovered that I was the speaker, he seemed embarrassed and shocked. At the close of the meeting I started to walk over to speak to him, but he turned and walked in the other direction. I felt that perhaps I had offended him; but when the attendance cards were collected, we discovered that he had indicated on his card that he had prayed to accept Jesus Christ as his Savior at that meeting!

The next morning I called him on the telephone. For the first time in eight years, I heard his voice. Not once during the eight years, had he returned my many messages. After talking briefly over the phone, we decided to meet for lunch at noon. At the restaurant, my neighbor told me that he had never been more sincere in his life than when he had prayed with me at the close of my message the day before. I counseled with him regarding the assurance of his salvation, the importance of starting to attend a good church, and the need to begin reading God's Word, the Bible. I also asked him to come to our CBMC prayer breakfast and Bible study the next morning. He eagerly agreed to attend.

Since we lived on the same street, we rode into town together. As I drove in, it was a joyful but strange experience, since for eight years I had not once been able to get his attention.

At the prayer breakfast, we passed out the prayer cards with the names of men who didn't know Christ— just as we usually do. My neighbor took two or three cards off the top of the pile. We divided into small groups, and when I asked him to join our group, I explained that it was not necessary for him to pray at all. I felt that he probably would not be comfortable praying, and I was trying to keep from embarrassing him. About this time he was looking at the cards in his hand, and noticed that one of them had his name on it. He asked why his name was on a card. I explained that for eight years we had prayed for him at each weekly breakfast, and that, in addition, I had been praying for him faithfully at home.

When it was his turn to pray, his prayer was one of the most beautiful that I have ever heard. It was simply, "Dear God, thank you for these men." He didn't pray in Jesus' name, he didn't say, "Amen," and he didn't pray for the other names on the cards he held. However, it was clear that he had been deeply touched by what he had heard and by what God had done for him. Having come to the Wednesday luncheon and then again on Friday, he had discovered that people cared. He and his wife (not the same one he had when he had failed to show at our home for dinner eight years before) did join, and became active in a church in our neighborhood. He has since gone on to heaven, but his wife is still active in her church!

In CBMC, we have a little tool that we call our "Ten Most Wanted" card. This little card, small enough to fit into a wallet or shirt pocket, is used by each of our members to list the names of ten people who do not know the Lord. We suggest that each member pray for every man on his card every day until they all come to know Jesus Christ. It is such a joy to be able to scratch a man's name off the list after he has committed his life to Christ. One CBMCer I recently talked with, told me that he was on his fourth card of brand-new names!

On more than one occasion, I have spoken at a CBMC meeting when a number of the lost acquaintances on a member's "Ten Most Wanted" card have been present and, following the close, God has given the increase. I'll never forget a dinner meeting in one city. One of our members had all ten of his "Ten Most Wanted" men in attendance, and afterward we discovered that an amazing nine out of that ten had marked their cards to indicate that they had accepted Jesus Christ! The CBMCer told me that he had prayed for some of those men for as long as twelve years. During that time, when some of the men on his list became saved, he would replace their names with those of other men who still did not know the Lord personally.

Through the years, the "Ten Most Wanted" card has served as an easy reminder of our continual need to pray for non-Christians we know, and the Lord has honored such faithfulness. I believe that this is something that every believer should be using as he seeks to serve God and to help show others how to find their way into His kingdom.

Of course, we realize that when a man gives his heart to the Lord, it is not only our prayers that are being answered. Often, God has used CBMC to answer the faithful prayers of those who may never have heard of our organization. I can think of one particular instance of this not too long ago.

I had been invited to speak at a CBMC luncheon in the Southeast. There was no head table, so I sat at a table near the microphone. A nicely dressed man, apparently in his late fifties, sat down beside me. He said that he was part owner of a car dealership in the city. I asked him if he had been to many CBMC luncheons, and he said no, that this was the first one he had ever attended.

As we and other men at the table talked, it was obvious that he was not the guest of the man seated on the other side of him, so I asked him who had brought him. He said, "My son brought me, and he would like me to become a Christian today." What a surprising statement! Never in all the years that I have been in CBMC had anyone ever said anything like that to me. I just commented, "Well, that would be nice, wouldn't it?"

After the meal, the program chairman got up to introduce me. The auto dealer did not associate me with the man being introduced, so when I got up to speak, he asked me, "Where are you going?"

"I'm the speaker," I said.

"You're the speaker?" he asked with surprise.

At the close of my talk, I asked the men to bow their heads and suggested that if they wanted to repent of their sins and personally claim the sin payment that Christ had provided on the cross, they could repeat a brief prayer with me. After the meeting, the man came up to me to tell me that he had sincerely prayed to ask Jesus to come into his life, and we spent a few moments in mutual rejoicing.

A few weeks later, my wife received a telephone call from Shirley LeTourneau, the wife of Roy LeTourneau, one of our veteran CBMC leaders. Shirley said she had had lunch that same week with a friend of hers asking about her ex-husband. The woman had heard that her former husband had received Christ at a CBMC luncheon where a fellow named Ted DeMoss had been the speaker, and she wanted to see if Shirley could find out any more information about it.

It seems that the woman, a Christian, had been divorced by her husband. He subsequently moved out of state, to the city where I had spoken; through God's sovereignty I had been seated next to him. Despite the divorce, and without any hope of ever becoming reconciled, the man's ex-wife had continued to pray for his salvation. One son had been active in one of our CBMCs in Michigan, and the other—the one who had brought his father to the luncheon—had just become involved with the CBMC in that city after having joined his father's business.

Here is one of the finest examples of unselfish, faithful prayer that I have ever heard of. It is also a clear illustration of the biblical truth that some plant, others water, but the Lord gives the increase.

There is no doubt that if we are to expect God's blessing on any of our Christian endeavors, we must commit these things to prayer. Whenever I see a local committee being used in wonderful ways by the Lord, I find that undergirding their efforts are faithful men speaking to God about unsaved men. Conversely, if one of our committees seems to be struggling, it often can be traced to a lack of prayer. The most well-planned outreach, held in the most attractive restaurant, with the most eye-appealing tables, the best-tasting food, and the most polished speaker, will fall short unless a firm foundation of prayer has been laid in advance.

Let us presume, however, that men have indeed been faithful in prayer. In addition, an outreach meeting has been well conducted, the gospel has been presented clearly, and the Holy Spirit has touched the hearts of many who have attended. Do we stop there? Not at all. In fact, in a very real sense, our work has just begun. Now is the time for the next step in our evangelizing/discipling process—what we refer to as "Follow-through."

CHAPTER FIVE

FOLLOW-THROUGH

Perpetual devotion to what a man calls his business is only to be sustained by perpetual neglect of many other things. Robert Louis Stevenson

But seek first His kingdom, and His righteousness; and all these things shall be added to you. Matthew 6:33

In sports, it is the follow-through that makes all the difference. Even if a baseball pitcher exhibits perfect form as he winds up, without proper follow-through he is likely to miss the target his catcher has given him. A championship tennis player knows that without a good follow-through, his serve may well end up in the net. Any avid golfer will tell you that a potential birdie can easily turn into a bogey (or worse) if he does not concentrate on his follow-through.

It is much the same in seeking to evangelize and disciple business and professional men for Jesus Christ. To terminate our efforts at the close of an outreach meeting, being satisfied with only a clear presentation of the gospel, is to leave the job partially done. There is still the responsibility of following through on our guests, offering to help them, regardless of where they may be in their spiritual pilgrimage.

There are some men who sincerely respond during our CBMC meetings, praying to commit their lives to Christ. Just as certainly, there are a few who, believing that they have sufficiently weighed the evidence, decide to reject Jesus Christ; we may never see them again at one of our functions. However, an overwhelming majority of our unsaved guests leave without having made either choice. Even if they did pray with the speaker, and marked a card with a "P" or an "X"—we have determined that in perhaps 90 percent of those cases, they are not truly born again. Those marks, more often than not, reflect feelings which range from general interest and openness toward spiritual matters to deeply felt cries for help. Rarely does a guest leave one of our meetings fully understanding all of what he has heard or truly comprehending what his prayer with the speaker meant.

Many times a man has told me he prayed with me at the close of a meeting "because you told me to!" For this reason, in CBMC one of our ministry activities has been labeled "Follow-through Visitation," which may range from calling on a man in his office, meeting with an outreach guest one-on-one over lunch, to inviting him and his wife, along with some other couples, to a private home for dinner or dessert and coffee. This gives us a chance to meet personally with a man, discussing his reaction to a speaker's message on a more intimate basis.

Over the years, our program of "office visitation" has been particularly successful. One might ask why we call on men in their offices instead of in their homes. There are several reasons. First of all, while a homemaker is most comfortable in her home, where she spends the majority of her time, we have found through experience that a businessman is most comfortable in his own office; after all, that is where *he* spends most of his time.

Second, in visiting a man in his home, we encounter three types of distractions: his wife, his children, and the television set. I remember talking to a very successful businessman in his home, and his wife kept interrupting. She would say things like, "See, I told you to quit drinking. If you became a Christian, we'd have more money to spend." He, in effect, told her, "Shut up!" We obviously weren't winning that man to Christ. It has gone that way with others. Eventually, we realized that the only way we would be able to have a worthwhile visit with a man was to isolate him so that he couldn't be distracted by his wife, children, television, the dog, or anything. We developed our office visitation program in response to this.

Basically, when we visit a man in his office, we try to ask him four questions: 1) Did you enjoy the meeting you attended? 2) Was there anything that you did not like about it? 3) What did you think about what the speaker had to say? 4) How did you relate personally to what the speaker said? During the course of those questions, we usually take a man's "spiritual temperature." By that we mean trying to determine whether a man is a Christian; and if he is a non-Christian, how open he is to discussing spiritual matters.

It may sound incredible, but in the years that I have been visiting men in their offices, I have never received a hostile reception. Of course, sometimes a man is busy and not available to see us; but generally men appreciate the fact that we have taken time out of our own busy schedules to stop by to see them.

For instance, I'll never forget making an office call with another man to visit a CPA who had recently attended one of our dinners. In the privacy of the man's office, the CPA told me that although he was glad to see us, there were two things that he would not discuss with anyone. When I inquired what those were, he responded that he was not interested in getting into a debate on the church or the Bible. I asked him why. He said that he had stopped attending church more than ten years earlier, and was not interested in anything that it had to offer. As far as the Bible was concerned, he said, "Anyone knows that disgruntled Jews wrote it."

I assured the accountant that I had not come by to discuss either issue, but rather to tell him about the greatest thing that ever happened in my life. I proceeded to share my personal testimony with him. His comment was "That's mighty nice, but I don't believe a bit of it." I asked him to tell me his view of what life is really all about. He told me that he had quit his job and was moving to Alaska, hoping to find the answer to that very question. My surprise at the news that he was leaving was evident, because he had thought that his boss had sent me in to see him. I assured him that the only reason I had stopped by was because he had been a guest at our CBMC dinner.

The accountant went on to explain that he had answered a blind ad in the *Wall Street Journal,* and was going to work as a CPA for a firm in Anchorage. He had never been to Alaska, so I told him that I had been there several times. I assured him that although the weather was cold and there would not be much daylight at that time of year, he would find the people in Anchorage essentially the same as those he knew in his hometown. The businessman seemed very disappointed to hear that he could travel that far and find nothing changed, except for the temperature and the number of daylight hours. However, he had already committed himself to go.

Before I left his office, I wished him well and also gave him a copy of the booklet, *The Reason Why.* I asked him to make a promise that not only would he read it as he flew to Anchorage the following week, but also that he would write me his thoughts about it soon after he arrived in the Great Land. As I was preparing to leave the office, I asked him if I could pray for him. He agreed, even though I suspect he was somewhat scared of what I might say. I prayed briefly that God would show him the truth of what he would be reading in that booklet about why Jesus Christ has the only answer to life.

Just a few weeks later I received a beautiful letter from him. He wrote that he had not only accepted Jesus Christ as his Savior after reading the booklet, but also had started reading the Bible and resumed attending church. He also stated that he already had a change of heart, was turning in his resignation to the Anchorage firm, and would be moving back to his hometown. Upon returning to the "lower forty-eight," he went through a personal development program we call "Operation Timothy" (to be covered in the next chapter) with an attorney, and even joined the local CBMC. This story of a man who changed from a skeptical non-Christian apparently uninterested in spiritual concerns to an active Christian, is one that has been duplicated over and over in CBMCs around the country.

Our office visitation program was developed in the early '70s. A veteran CBMCer and I had been discussing the need for an effective follow-up program for our guests. He suggested that I go to a city, away from my hometown of Chattanooga, to see if I could develop a program to visit men effectively. I said, "Where do you have in mind?"

He said, "New York City—Manhattan." Now I have to admit, that's about as tough a place as you can go to, since two million men and women travel to New York to work each day and they don't even live there.

In spite of that, we decided to go. Over the next months I spent several weeks there. The first time I went with one other man, and the second time with three others. All day long, from morning until night, we were calling on men in their offices to share Jesus Christ with them—during business hours, with no appointments. We never telephoned ahead of time. After spending a total of about one month in New York,

I went to St. Louis with another man for two weeks. Just through hit-and-miss and trial-and-error, we developed a simple program that works.

When we started, I had felt strongly that we needed an effective follow-up program. By the time we were through, I was sure of it. We had some of the most unusual calls. One fellow told us, "I've been to three CBMC meetings. I was converted three different times—at all three luncheons." (At that point, he didn't know the word *saved*.) He said, "I've always marked on the card that I would like to know more about what's been said. I had never heard from anyone. I decided that you guys didn't mean business, and nine months ago I said I would never go to another meeting. You're the first men from CBMC who have ever showed up here."

On other occasions we called on incredibly busy men. Many times men interrupted their schedules, occasionally even breaking away from meetings already in progress, to talk with me and the CBMCer that I was with.

I recall one particular time we went to see one man, and the receptionist said, "I'm very sorry, but without an appointment you cannot see him." I asked her to please get him on the phone and tell him that I was with Christian Business Men (which is the approach we use). "I'd like to see him just for a few minutes."

She replied, "I'm sorry, but he won't be able to see you." I finally prevailed upon her to call him, and she did, simply telling her boss that two men from Christian Business Men were there to see him.

"What does he want?" the executive asked her.

"I don't know," she answered, and she handed me the phone.

I said "Mr. Thompson, I'm with Christian Business Men, and we'd like to see you just for a few minutes. Can we come to your office?"

We were on the eleventh floor, and his office was on the fourteenth floor. He told me that we could not come up, since he had a room full of people, but if we could wait a few minutes he would come down to see us. I later discovered that this man was the personnel director and a senior vice-president on the New York Stock Exchange with more than 40,000 employees.

A short time later he got off the elevator, introduced himself to us, and asked, "What do you want to know?" I told him that I had a couple of questions to ask him.

"Well, if it's going to take a lot of time, I don't have much time," he responded. I assured him that we would try to be as brief as possible.

I told him that it was my understanding that he had attended one of our meetings, and he confirmed that he had. I asked him, "What did you like about the meeting? What did you like about what you heard?"

He replied, "It was the most fantastic story I ever heard in my entire life."

"What didn't you like about what you heard?" He answered simply: "That fellow never explained how I could have it happen in my own life. If you want to know the truth, I left that meeting in my office today to come down here because I want what the speaker had. I hope you fellows can help me find what that man had."

This very busy man, who had left an important meeting and had stated flatly that he did not have much time, sat with us in a public lobby for about one hour and fifteen minutes discussing what the Bible says about peace, the meaning of life, and eternal life. We had the joy of seeing that man come to know Jesus Christ.

Later, I learned that the speaker at the meeting he had attended had given a clear explanation of the gospel, and had invited the men to pray with him to receive Jesus Christ. But this executive didn't understand what the speaker was saying, since he knew so little about the Bible. In fact, we found out that the man did not even own a Bible. We didn't have to do it, but after we left the building that day, we went to a bookstore and bought him a Bible. We arranged to meet him for lunch the next day, gave him the Bible, and suggested a study outline to help him get started in reading it. We also gave his name to a local CBMCer to follow up on him further.

One of the great things we have discovered about this approach to follow-through is that you can use it for church visitation or in conjunction with activities sponsored by an evangelistic Christian organization. You just ask the visitor what he liked (about the church service, the meeting, or whatever the event might have been), what he did not like, what he thought of the speaker's message, and how he related to it personally. There are no tricks or gimmicks, just sincere interest and concern for the person and where he (or she) is spiritually.

Perhaps what impresses me most as I make these office visits around the country is how open businessmen are to discussing the claims of Jesus Christ. Anyone who states that business and professional men cannot be reached for Christ just hasn't tried very hard to reach them.

I recall another office call I made that illustrates this point. The businessman was in his sixties. Twice during our conversation, the man drove his fist onto his glass-topped desk with such force that I was afraid the glass would shatter. Both times he said emphatically, "I need help. Where can I find someone to help me?" He knew he was not a Christian. In fact, he said that he had only recently encountered the first Christians he had ever recognized as such. His daughter and son-in-law in another city had both given their hearts to Jesus Christ and had begun sharing their faith with him.

After we had spent thirty or forty minutes explaining the gospel to him, the businessman agreed to become involved in CBMC's four-lesson Bible discussion series that we call *First Steps.* (I will also discuss it in the next chapter.) I was already involved in Bible study and discipleship programs with a number of other people, so I paired him up with another CBMCer in our city who started meeting with him faithfully. Three months after that initial visit, I had the unusual privilege of seeing him commit his life to Christ after he had heard me give my testimony at a luncheon.

While I was speaking, I had noticed him in the audience. In fact, I had been told that he probably would be there. Following the meeting, he came up to me and gave me a big bear hug. With tears in his eyes, the businessman told me that for the first time he had sincerely accepted Jesus Christ as his personal Savior.

What about the man who does understand an outreach speaker's message, and does sincerely pray for Jesus Christ to come into his life? Does he still need to be followed up? Well, let's look at it this way: When a baby is born, we don't put a diaper on him, pat him on the head, and send him off into the world, do we? Of course not. We shouldn't treat new Christians that way, either.

The Apostle Paul stated it this way in his first letter to the church in Corinth: "And I, brethren, could not speak to you as to spiritual men, but as to men of flesh, as to babes in Christ. I gave you milk to drink, not solid food; for you were not yet able to receive it ... " (1 Corinthians 3:1, 2).

The Bible makes it clear that Christians have the responsibility not only for evangelizing the lost, but also for discipling the newer members of the faith, "with all wisdom teaching and admonishing one another ... " (Colossians 3:16).

How do we go about doing that? In the next chapter, I will be telling you about a couple of tools that we have used very effectively in CBMC: *First Steps* and *Operation Timothy.*

CHAPTER SIX

OPERATION TIMOTHY

God helps those that help themselves.
Benjamin Franklin

And the things which you have heard from me in the presence of many witnesses, these entrust to faithful men who will be able to teach others also.
2 Timothy 2:2

While visiting the accounting firm which handles our auditing, I was asked to stop by and see one of the CPAs who was employed there. Since she had never done any work on either my personal account or the books of CBMC of USA, I was somewhat surprised when I was told that she had asked to see me.

Almost immediately as I entered her office, the woman started to explain that she and her husband, a banking executive in the same city, needed help. She told me a little of her past and shared that both she and her husband had been married before. They feared they might be headed for another marital disaster. The accountant had heard that I was taking the senior partner in the firm through a program called "Operation Timothy," in which we discussed the teachings of the Bible. She candidly stated that perhaps something like that could help in her situation.

As it happened, I was preparing to leave for Australia that same afternoon and would be out of town for six weeks. However, I promised that my wife and I would be glad to meet with both of them after we returned. We left Chattanooga that same afternoon, and late that evening arrived in San Francisco. As I emptied my pockets, I discovered I still had two tickets for the out-reach luncheon the next week in Chattanooga. I decided to mail them to the accountant, asking her and her husband to attend as my guests. I did not find out until I returned to the United States a month and a half later that they had attended the meeting. Not only that, but they also prayed to give their hearts to Jesus Christ!

I called the accountant the week we got back in town and arranged to begin meeting with her and her husband at 6:30 in the morning, so it would not conflict with their busy schedules. The day before we were to meet, she called. "I forgot to ask you," the woman said. "What should we bring?"

"Well, bring a notepad, a pencil—and a Bible."

She said she did not have a Bible, but then said, "I think my husband has one, but it's old. I don't know if it's still good." Concealing my amusement, I assured her that it would be.

To some of us, her comment may sound strange. But it shouldn't. Look at it from the perspective of the modern, secular business person. Every day, laws are being changed, regulations are being revised, procedures are being updated. To the secular business person, why shouldn't the Scriptures also be altered to keep up with the times? After all, doesn't a "new Bible" come out almost every year?

That marked the beginning of what was to be a joyous and enlightening relationship between me and my wife, and the other couple. Generally, when I begin discipling someone, helping him to understand the Scriptures and how to apply them to his daily life, I prefer to start with an introductory Bible discussion series we have called *First Steps*. In these four lessons we discuss basic issues such as "Is the Bible Credible?" and "The Person of Jesus Christ." This helps to establish a foundation on which to build.

That first morning the accountant and her husband, whom I had never met, arrived on time and we started on the first lesson in *First Steps.* I had brought along a new, modern translation of the Bible *(NIV)* so they both could have one, and I suggested that we start by each reading a Scripture verse. I showed them the index, so they could find the various books of the Bible.

I suggested that we each read a verse, explain what we think it means, then tell how it applies to our lives today.

When it was the accountant's turn, she read 2 Timothy 3:16, "All Scripture is God-breathed and is useful for teaching, rebuking, correcting and training in righteousness."

"I didn't know that God wrote a book!" she exclaimed. "That means, then, that I can believe everything the Bible says!"

As years pass, it is easy for us as Christians to grow complacent, to lose the childlike wonder that we had when we first began our relationship with the Lord. Believe me, it is so exciting to watch a new Christian begin to learn and grow in Christ. To see such sincere, uninhibited enthusiasm for the living Lord is contagious. If you are a dry, dispirited Christian who has lost his zeal—and you want to stay that way—then let me warn you: never disciple a new Christian. You're likely to catch what he has!

Since that first week, it became a real adventure to work with this sharp young accountant and her banker husband. Each week, we would see them both growing in understanding and love for the Lord. In addition, it was not long before we began to see that they had a real burden for their unsaved friends. Many of them were facing the same struggles, and this couple was eager to tell them that they had finally discovered the answer.

Several months later, the couple was attending another of our outreach luncheons. The woman approached one of our CBMCers and asked if he had one of those "little books."

"You mean *Operation Timothy?*" he responded.

"No, the little books you use when you visit people in their offices. We brought some guests with us, and they need to see them." The books she was referring to were *Steps to Peace with God* and *The Reason Why*. These people have such an eagerness to serve God. I hope no one ever tells them that they're not supposed to be like that!

In my opinion, one of the greatest needs of Christians today is discipleship. A decision to accept Jesus Christ as Savior and Lord is the important and essential first step in an individual's Christian life. But it is just that—a new beginning. As I have traveled around the country, speaking to groups of business and professional men, it has not been uncommon for a man to walk up to me after a meeting and say, "OK, I sincerely prayed with you to ask Jesus Christ into my life. Now what do I do?"

Too often, our response is simply to point him to the nearest good, Bible-based church and encourage him to be there at the next Sunday morning service. I wholeheartedly urge new believers to join in worship and fellowship with other Christians. But it is wrong to assume that a new person in Christ will instantly acquire a clear understanding of how he is to live as the "new creation" described in 2 Corinthians 5:17. In most cases, the best way for the new Christian to get off to a good start in his walk with the Lord is by taking the "personal approach," spending time, one-on-one, with a mature Christian man or woman or couple— discussing the Bible, and especially how we are to apply its principles to our everyday lives.

This is not a case of personal preference; over and over, it is the way God uses to train up His men and to prepare them for the important tasks they are to perform. When Jesus Christ left His disciples after His resurrection, He was confident that this handful of men had been ably prepared for the mission of spreading the gospel throughout the world. After all, He had spent the final three years of His earthly life in intimate fellowship with them.

After the Apostle Paul met Christ on the road to Damascus, God brought a man—Barnabas—into his life to serve as his mentor, guiding and training him until the day when he was ready to march off for God on his own. We also have the loving, challenging letters from Paul to one of his disciples, Timothy, in which he shared his own life experiences with this younger man in Christ.

I have met many men who told me about how they had given their lives to the Lord earlier in life, but did not start to grow as Christians until years later. Frequently they say something like, "If only someone had come to me years ago and showed me how to read the Bible and understand it, how to pray, and how to share my faith!"

Recognizing this need, in CBMC we have developed two tools which have been very useful in this discipling process. *First Steps* is designed for new Christians with little or no Bible knowledge and for non-Christians who are searching for spiritual truths. The other study, which we have named *Operation Timothy,* is more intensive, consisting of twelve lessons. It also incorporates Scripture memory verses into each lesson.

First Steps has been particularly exciting, not only for me, but for many of our men in CBMC. In fact, a number of churches have begun using this course in a variety of ways. In many cases, *First Steps* has helped non-Christians confront the issue of who Jesus Christ is and where they are in relation to the Bible's teachings on salvation. Often for the first time they understand their need to make a personal decision to accept Christ and his substitutionary payment for their sins. For others, going through *First Steps* has helped them to conceptualize the significance of a decision they had made at an outreach meeting, or perhaps at another time.

One activity Edith and I like to sponsor after an outreach meeting is what we call a "home dinner party." We invite some couples who have attended one of these functions, asking them to a buffet supper so that we might talk with them about what we heard at the CBMC event. A remarkably high percentage of the people we invite will come and are actually interested in discussing what they heard at a luncheon or dinner.

As the evening comes to an end, I always tell the guests that I will be calling each of the men in the room the following day to see if they would be interested in coming to a four-lesson Bible discussion *(First Steps)*. On the average, about half of the people at our dinner parties will return to our home for the four discussion topics, even though often we will spend two or three sessions on one of the lessons.

One of our dinner parties proved to be a particular source of joy. Many of the couples agreed to participate in the Bible discussion. Over the next three months, every one of them made a profession of faith in Jesus Christ. It is so exciting to get to know people like these individually, to see their growing interest in biblical truths, and to observe the working of the Holy Spirit in their hearts as they become convicted of their need for the Savior.

Again, all we are doing is making ourselves available to be used by God. Each of the people we invited has marked an outreach registration card, indicating that he has prayed with the speaker to ask Christ into his life. Often we discover that the person did not fully understand what he was doing when he repeated the prayer, but at least we know there is some openness to spiritual matters. Some continue to tell me they prayed with the speaker because he told them to! These two Bible discussion series give them an opportunity to talk further about their concerns, either one-on-one or in small groups.

Why are these discussions so effective? The Bible tells us, "For the Word of God is living and active and sharper than any two-edged sword, and piercing as far as the division of soul and spirit, of both joints and marrow, and able to judge the thoughts and intentions of the heart" (Hebrews 4:12). Indeed it is! Unless a person who indicated an interest in spiritual things gets into the Word of God, I don't see any hope for him ever to grow or mature spiritually.

We always encourage such people to begin attending strong, evangelical churches that stand for the Bible as God's Word and for Christ as the only way to God. However, I have seen on numerous occasions that because of something in a person's past, it may take him several weeks or even months before he is willing to go back to church—if in fact he ever attended previously. So, during this interim period, it is important that we try to get the person into the Word. Through the Scriptures, God will show him his need for worship and fellowship with other believers.

As I have explained, we view *First Steps* as just that: a very basic introduction to the Bible, particularly in what it tells us about Jesus Christ and our relationship to God. However, it serves merely as a starting point. After taking a person through *First Steps,* we feel it is really time to get him started in the discipling process. It is at this point that we find *Operation Timothy* to be a very effective—and challenging—tool for teaching.

I have had many exciting experiences using *Operation Timothy,* and it has given me the opportunity to get to know dozens of wonderful people. One particular couple who attended one of our banquets comes to mind. The wife had become a Christian two years before. Her husband, however, had reluctantly gone to the dinner, considering what little he knew of the teachings of the Bible to be utter foolishness.

The speaker that night talked much longer than we prefer; he went on for one hour and twenty minutes! Surprisingly, at the close, the reluctant guest marked the registration card to indicate that he had prayed with the speaker, inviting Jesus Christ into his life for the very first time. He had made no attempt to conceal his response, so I asked the man if he understood what he had done. He frankly answered, "Not really, but you know, he did tell us to pray with him." I don't mean to sound sarcastic, but I suspect that if the speaker had asked the guests to pray to Santa Claus or the Easter Bunny, this man would have followed the instructions.

Talking with this man further, I discovered that he managed a company branch for a large national firm, overseeing 110 employees. He obviously was a sharp, capable individual. I asked him what he knew about the Bible. He commented that he knew nothing about the Bible. Not only that, but he could not remember going to church more than one or two times in his life, except for weddings and funerals.

I suggested that it might be fun to look into the Bible to see what it has to say. To encourage him, I pointed out that we might discover that it has a message for the top-level businessman in today's economy. Curious, he agreed to meet with me from 6:30 to 8:00 the following Monday morning. At that time, we did not yet have the *First Steps* series, so we began our meeting by discussing the initial lesson in *Operation Timothy*, which deals with the assurance of salvation. We didn't quite complete that lesson, but the executive agreed to come back the next week to finish it. I placed two conditions on coming back the next Monday: he had to finish the lesson at home and he had to memorize the corresponding verses for that chapter, 1 John 5:11–13: "And the witness is this, that God has given us eternal life, and this life is in His Son. He who has the Son has the life; he who does not have the Son of God does not have the life. These things I have written to you who believe in the name of the Son of God, in order that you may know that you have eternal life."

To find out what his reaction was to what we had discussed, before we left I asked the man what he thought about it. I have to commend him on his candidness. He simply said, "I don't believe a word of it."

Fortunately, there were other lessons and other discussions in the weeks that followed. We continued to meet regularly, and the businessman was a model student. He always had his required verses memorized, and he never failed to have his work done in the *Operation Timothy* workbook. Amazingly, he still wasn't a Christian. He didn't even think he was a Christian. Yet we had some of the most stimulating, challenging discussions that I've ever had with anyone.

Our progress was slow, and after nearly three months of meeting almost every week, we had only begun with lesson four. I was stumped in trying to determine a way to move him from "head knowledge" to "heart knowledge." One day, I felt impressed to give him a copy of the booklet *The Reason Why*.

Two or three days later, the executive called me very early in the morning to say, "Ted, I want you to be the first to know that I'm a Christian." Then he asked why the author of *Operation Timothy* had waited to introduce *The Reason Why* so late in the program. He said, "If you had given that to me the first week, it would have been different. I would have accepted Jesus Christ weeks ago."

I didn't have the heart to tell my friend that *The Reason Why* was not even included as part of *Operation Timothy*. Had I given it to him earlier, he might have made a commitment to the Lord earlier. Then again, perhaps not. Romans 10:17 tells us that "faith comes from hearing, and hearing by the Word of Christ." I am confident that it was the Word of God, not a booklet, that God used to bring this man to Christ. The Lord simply used *The Reason Why* as the specific vehicle to help him reach the decision. However, since he had been in God's Word for those many weeks, he made that commitment fully understanding its implications.

We continued in *Operation Timothy* over the succeeding months, eventually completing it over the course of one year. It is such a joy to see him still walking with Jesus Christ today—several years later—with a very evident desire to reach others for his Lord.

In talking with him recently, he informed me that there has not been one day since the day he became a Christian that he hasn't prayed for me. Talk about fringe benefits! That is one that only eternity can fully measure.

First Steps. Operation Timothy. These are simple tools that I have found effective in exposing new and prospective Christians to the truths of the Bible. There are many other excellent tools, and other methods. The important thing is that we have an approach of some sort that we find comfortable.

A student once approached the great D. L. Moody and told him, "I don't like your method for sharing your faith."

"That's fine," Dr. Moody replied. "What is your method?" The student admitted that he did not have one. "Well, I like mine better than yours."

The same principle applies in discipleship. Effectiveness in carrying out the Lord's work does not depend upon a specific tool or method. But when God presents us with people to whom we can minister, we do need some sort of plan to take advantage of the opportunities.

The other key element is time. You can't disciple a person in a day, a week, or even a month. Just as people differ in interests, abilities, and personal tastes, they also differ in the amount of time they require before they reach some degree of spiritual maturity and independence. But I have found that to be truly effective in discipling another person, seeing to it that he is clearly growing and prospering in his relationship with the Lord, generally takes six months, a year, sometimes even longer.

Our task is not to operate an assembly line for Christians. The Scriptures give no guidelines for mass production; God's way is one man at a time. We also must remember that the timing is God's, not ours. He uses us in this discipleship process, but it is He who is doing the work! Technology has dramatically speeded up the pace of living in our society, but there is no such thing as "instant disciples." God still works the same way He did 2,000 years ago: day by day, week after week. If we are patient, and wait upon the Lord, He will see to it that we bear fruit that remains (John 15:16).

CHAPTER SEVEN

THE LIFESTYLE OF A CHRISTIAN BUSINESSMAN

For life in general, there is but one decree: youth is a blunder, manhood a struggle, old age a regret.
Benjamin Disraeli

But in your hearts acknowledge Christ as the holy Lord. Always be prepared to give an answer to everyone who asks you to give the reason for the hope that you have. But do this with gentleness and respect.... 1 Peter 3:15, 16 *(NIV)*

Over the years, I have had countless discussions with Christians—pastors and laypeople—about evangelism. Many of them perceive witnessing as something you do for a couple of hours, one night a week. There is nothing wrong with designating a week night specifically for sharing your faith with others. But I have found that evangelism is not something you do, but rather, something you live. In recent years, the term "lifestyle evangelism" has gained wide acceptance. I wholeheartedly approve, because I have found that being a witness for the Lord Jesus Christ is something you demonstrate through your life every day. Indeed, for the committed Christian, evangelism is a way of life.

As the Scripture passage at the beginning of this chapter states, we must "always be prepared to give an answer" in defense of our faith. Like a physician, we are "on call" twenty-four hours a day. If we are to be ambassadors for Christ, we have to accomplish it on His terms, according to His scheduling, not just when we feel like it or when it is convenient—or because it's "visitation night."

I did not come by this understanding easily. Just as I first was shown how to share my faith effectively, I learned this principle of being always prepared by observing the model and example of others. Perhaps one of the most memorable incidents occurred once while I was driving back to Chattanooga with several other men from a meeting that we had attended in Washington, D. C. On the way back, we were scheduled to speak at a church in southwestern Virginia for the Sunday morning service.

This meant that we had to get up early and drive hard to be sure to arrive in time for Sunday school and church. Fearful that we might not get there on time, and really not knowing how far we had to travel that morning, we decided to skip breakfast. Our concern had been unwarranted, since we arrived at the church forty-five minutes before the start of Sunday school. Fortunately, we noticed that a restaurant was open across the street from the church, so the four of us walked over to have a belated breakfast.

We had been in the restaurant only a moment when one of the men in our group disappeared. Wondering where he had gone, I began looking around the restaurant. I soon discovered that after going through the cafeteria line, Harry had taken his tray and joined an obviously crippled man who was sitting alone in a booth on the far side of the room. This man was as badly deformed as any man I have ever seen. It seemed that it was all he could do to feed himself. One leg was much shorter than the other, one of his arms was withered, and he had such a severe curvature of the spine that his head almost rested on the table. I could not imagine how my fellow CBMCer could have known this unfortunate individual.

Before we had finished our breakfast, Harry came over to our table and said that he wanted to introduce me to a brand-new Christian. A bit puzzled, I walked across the restaurant with him and met this man, who seemed amazingly radiant. As I talked with the man, he related a tale of misery that I could hardly comprehend. He was a ward of the city, and had been for many, many years. All his meals were provided free in that restaurant; and day after day, month after month, he went there for breakfast, lunch, and dinner. In all those years, Harry was the very first man that he could remember sitting down to eat with him. He had never had a friend.

When Harry had joined him and showed him genuine love and compassion, this man was overwhelmed. Then Harry, his first-ever friend, told him about his own best Friend, the Lord Jesus Christ. The man learned that in spite of his woeful physical condition, he could begin experiencing the abundant life immediately—and forever. Through Harry's simple act of concern, the crippled man recognized that there was something very different about him. He was ready to respond to the words of the gospel, because he had already seen it in action.

Matthew 5:16 says, "Let your light shine before men in such a way that they may see your good works, and glorify your Father who is in heaven." I don't believe that I have ever seen a better example of that passage put into practice.

In another chapter in Matthew, Jesus is talking to His disciples. He tells them, "Follow me, and I will make you fishers of men." As He often did, the Lord was using an analogy that His followers could understand from their daily lives. Several of them were fishermen, and one obvious principle which they practiced was to go where the fish were. The same principle applies to us as Christians, as we seek to share our faith with those who do not know Jesus Christ.

To Harry, in that southwestern Virginia restaurant, it meant walking across a room to spend some caring moments with a lonely, miserable man. For the rest of us, it may mean getting to know a neighbor whom we have successfully ignored for years. It may mean spending time with a work associate whose lifestyle does not particularly appeal to us. Or it may mean breaking away from our comfortable, familiar "holy huddles" of Christian friends to reach out into the non-Christian realm.

Please do not misunderstand. Christian fellowship is fine; in fact, it is essential if we are to continue as properly functioning members of the Body of Christ. But the Bible tells us that we are "the salt of the earth ... the light of the world" (Matthew 5:13, 14). As Rebecca Pippert has said in her book, *Out of the Saltshaker and into the World,*[1] salt is of no value if it is kept inside the saltshaker. In the same way, we are to shine our light into the world, not hide it under a bushel, or within the safe confines of our church buildings.

How are we to reach out to the non-Christians around us? On more than one occasion, I have had CBMC members approach me and admit apologetically, "But I don't know any non-Christians." In one sense, such a statement sounds amazing, given our estimate that 90 percent of the business and professional men in America do not have a personal relationship with Jesus Christ. Yet, in another respect, it is not all that surprising. It has been said that on the average, within two years of becoming a Christian, a man has lost all his non-Christian friends. I am convinced that in many cases it does not take that long. Often a new Christian has severed all his non-Christian associations within six months!

Of course, when a person gives his life to Christ many changes occur. Some friends may not appreciate the difference and might cease to call or come by to visit. For the new Christian, there may be some activities that he used to do regularly as a non-Christian, but

---

[1] Rebecca Manley Pippert, *Out of the Saltshaker and into the World* (Downers Grove, Ill.: InterVarsity Press, 1979), p. 11.

finds he can no longer participate in because they are not consistent with the Christian life. Associations in those areas may also be severed. I am convinced, however, that it is unnecessary to totally disassociate ourselves from the non-Christian world. The Lord Jesus gives us our best example. He who knew no sin spent most of His time associating with sinners. In fact, one of the major criticisms directed toward Him by the Jewish priests and scribes concerned the men He chose as His companions. His response was "I did not come to call the righteous, but sinners" (Matthew 9:13).

Our challenge as Christians is to remain in the world, but "not of the world" (John 17:14–18). We need to be able to identify with those who are without Christ, but also realize that our lives are to demonstrate a radically different perspective. In his book, *Lifestyle Evangelism,* Joe Aldrich gives an excellent presentation of what he terms the "process of evangelism." [2] I will not attempt to summarize in a few sentences what he explains so well in detail.

However, in CBMC we were so convinced that the evangelism process is consistent with the teachings of the Scriptures that we developed the unique "Lifestyle Evangelism Seminar." This seminar explains how to cultivate caring relationships with non-Christians, communicate the gospel clearly, and effectively use your personal testimony. Since it started in January of 1982, thousands of men and women have participated in this program and have gained new insights into how they can be used by God to reach out to those around them. Many churches around the country are also using this training, reporting fruitful results.

In my own case, I started sharing my Christian faith long before the Lifestyle Evangelism Seminar was conceived. If I were to summarize my own philosophy of

[2] Joseph C. Aldrich, *Lifestyle Evangelism* (Portland, Ore.: Multnomah Press, 1978), p. 26.

witnessing in just a few words, it would be to "think lost." Too often we can get caught up by Christian friends, Christian jargon, and our own "spirituality." In fact, it has been said that we can become so heavenly minded that we are no earthly good! I find if we make a conscious effort to seek to relate to the unsaved person—whether talking to someone individually, or addressing a group—some will respond. We need to be sensitive to where they are and what their needs are, not what we would like them to be.

One time I was sharing with some pastors about how Edith and I use our home for outreach purposes. I told them of a time when we invited eighteen people (who, as far as we knew, were not Christians) to our home for a buffet supper. We did invite one other Christian couple, because they wanted to observe how we used our home for evangelism. I explained to the pastors how we shared Jesus Christ in this type of setting and how we had started a Bible study as a result. In this instance, eventually we saw nine of the eighteen come to know Christ and get involved with local churches.

After my explanation, one of the clergymen asked if he could raise a concern that bothered him somewhat. He asked, "What would you do if someone lit up a cigarette in your home?" My honest answer was that I would hand the man an ashtray. The pastor then questioned whether my home was committed to the Lord. I intended no sarcasm by my response, which was simply that my home indeed was dedicated to serving the Lord; it was not, however, dedicated to stamping out tobacco.

You see, I think there really comes a time when we must decide how we are going to serve the Lord. I don't believe the Lord wants me to spend my life seeking to blot out the world's vices or to persuade people to give up habits which I find unacceptable. Christ Himself did not come to change our habits; He came to save individuals who would call upon His name. If we are to dedicate our lives to the Word of God and to others, we're going to have to meet with people where they are. If there are changes needed in their lives, the Holy Spirit will take care of those areas *after* they come to know Jesus Christ.

In CBMC, we often use the motto, "Today Sam Smith trusted Jesus Christ because yesterday he trusted Pete Jones." The implication is that until we earn the right to be heard, there really is not much chance that we *will* be heard. In other words, we have to *be* good news to the people we meet before we can tell them the Good News.

For the Christian who is burdened for lost souls, it is indeed a challenge to see that his "walk" is consistent with his talk. I would not begin to claim that I have always been successful in this respect; in fact, I have fallen short more times than I can remember. But I have discovered that non-Christians have a knack for separating the talkers from the doers. Experts tell us that more than 60 percent of all communication is nonverbal. Therefore, we are warned that the old saying "Do as I say, not as I do" will not work as we try to relate to the lost world. In fact, it has been brought to my attention more than once that non-Christians expect us to live by a higher standard than we set for ourselves!

One time I was seeking to help a friend with an alcohol problem that was disrupting his entire life. He was fairly open to the gospel. He even attended church with me a few times. One day he came by my office and asked if I would walk with him to a restaurant a block from my office in the downtown area of our city. Wondering what he had in mind, I agreed.

He pointed out an attractive woman seated at a table by the window. She was drinking a beer. My friend had been walking by the restaurant, and since she was sitting in plain view, he had seen her. He recognized her as a woman who sang in our church choir.

"You've been telling me that Jesus Christ can help me overcome my drinking problem, yet here is a woman from your church, openly drinking a beer," he said angrily. I tried to offer an explanation, but there was no hope. For all I know, that might have been the only beer the woman had all year, but her actions made an impact on this man.

I was no longer able to discuss the gospel with my friend. Judging from what he had seen, he felt the church had nothing to offer him. Granted, this might have merely been his excuse for rejecting the gift that God was offering him. Nevertheless, this spoke to me about our responsibility for representing the Lord around the clock.

As I read the Gospel accounts of how the Lord Jesus related to lost people whom he encountered, I am impressed with the genuine love and compassion he exhibited toward them. Joe Aldrich has summed up this concept well: "People don't care how much you know, until they know how much you care." [3] How true that is. Too often when we witness to people—at a social gathering, on an airplane, or in any other setting—we have a tendency to approach them as evangelism "projects," without demonstrating a sincere concern for their needs, for the areas in which they are hurting. John 3:16 says, "For God so loved the world, that He gave His only begotten Son. . . ."As we share our faith with others, we need to be able to communicate this love to them.

I'll never forget the time that my phone rang, about five minutes to ten in the morning. I had been away from my business for a number of days, so mail was piled high on my desk and people were waiting to meet with me. I'll admit that I was not overjoyed to have a

---

[3] Ibid., p. 35.

friend call and ask me to go downtown immediately to see a man in a hotel room who was "in trouble."

"Why can't *you* go?" I asked him. He explained that he was to be the speaker at a meeting in just five minutes; besides, he felt "the Lord wanted me to go"! I wasn't convinced of that, but I did call the fellow in the hotel to see what the problem was.

When the man answered the phone, he sounded more depressed than anyone I had ever tried to engage in a conversation. Frankly, I wasn't sure what to say. I told him that he did not know me, but I wanted to talk with him. When he asked me, "What do you want to talk to me about?" I used an answer I find usually works.

"I understand you need a friend," I responded. As soon as I said that, the man in the hotel—Ed—began sobbing uncontrollably while he was trying to talk with me. Finally, he managed to get out a few words that I could understand: "I need a friend more than anything in the whole world." Forgetting about my business obligations, I told him that I would drive to see him right away. He asked me how long it would take to get to the hotel. I explained that it would take me thirty minutes, even if I left right away. Quietly, he said that I shouldn't bother to come. When I asked him where he was going, he said that he would be dead in thirty minutes.

I had heard many drunks threaten to jump out of hotel windows or to take their lives in some other way, but this man obviously was not drunk, nor was he joking. I informed him that I was a very busy man and I was not interested in wasting thirty minutes to drive downtown to see a corpse. I told him that I was going to hang up the telephone and I would get there as quickly as I could. I also said that I wanted him to wait until after I met him before doing anything drastic. I hung up the phone without waiting for a response and walked out to the parking lot, only to discover that I didn't have a car. I had forgotten that it was in the shop for repairs!

I borrowed someone else's car and headed for downtown. As I walked up the hotel corridor, I looked at my watch. It was exactly 10:30. When I got to the man's room, the door was ajar a couple of inches. I pushed it open, not knowing what I would see. Sitting on the edge of the bed was a well dressed man, his face in his hands. I could not tell whether his eyes were open or closed; if they were open, he was staring at the floor. He did not look up at me, although I was sure that he had heard me enter the room.

The bed did not appear to have been slept in, and there was no luggage in view. The only thing in the room that I noticed was a bottle of sleeping pills, the largest I have ever seen, on top of the dresser, within his reach. Apparently, it had not been opened. I sat down next to the man on the side of the bed, put one arm around him, and asked if he wanted to talk about what was troubling him. He proceeded to tell me a lengthy story about how as a young man he had deserted his wife and first child in Chattanooga more than nineteen years before, when the infant was just six months old. He told me that he had not attempted to see the boy since then. He had never written to him, nor sent him a birthday card, a Christmas present, or anything else. Sitting in the hotel room, Ed sobbingly told me that the day before, he had seen his son for the first time in those nineteen years—lying in a coffin. His son had been serving in the Navy, and was killed in an automobile accident.

As he related this story to me, which took about half an hour, Ed had not looked up at me once. With his face still buried in his hands, Ed spoke slowly, informing me that it was his plan to take his own life, so that he could go wherever his son was and tell him he was sorry. I quickly pointed out that things might not work out as he planned, that he might not go to where his son was. He didn't seem to understand, so I explained to him that the Bible clearly tells us that some people go to heaven when they die and some go to hell. He told me that he really didn't believe that, but asked me who goes to which place.

At this point, I shared with him my entire testimony of how Jesus Christ had changed my life and had given me purpose and direction, a sense of values, and a thousand other things besides. I asked Ed if he had married again. He told me about his second wife and the two children he would be leaving behind on the West Coast. Even with this family depending upon him, he felt that he had to try to right this wrong to his son by punching out of this world and moving on to the next one. There, he figured, he could get some time with his first son. Confused thinking? You bet! But that is what sin and guilt can do to an individual.

When I had told him everything I could think of to tell him, I suggested that we go have lunch together. He said in a shocked voice, "Are you crazy? I'm not hungry!" It was only then that he looked up, and I saw his face for the first time. He might have thought I was crazy, but I could see from his face that *he* was not. I begged him to go to lunch with me, but he told me to go ahead by myself. When I asked him what he was going to do, he simply said, "You know what I'm going to do."

I decided to call upon his sense of obligation. I pointed out that I had already given him more than an hour of my time, and the least he could do was give me an hour of *his* time. I grabbed him by the arm and physically tried to make him come with me, even though he was a much stronger man than I am. Reluctantly, he walked along with me. We took the elevator down from his room and went to my car. It just happened this was the day of our midweek CBMC luncheon. I would not say it was coincidence, because long ago I learned that, with God, nothing is by chance.

We went to the restaurant where the luncheon was to be held. When he saw all the other men there, Ed was disturbed, to say the least. He asked me who they were. I answered him honestly, telling him that once a month I have lunch with this group, which is an organization called Christian Business Men. Ed said he wanted to go back to the hotel, and I said that we would—as soon as we ate. In fact, I told him I would make him a deal. I said, "If you'll sit here until one o'clock, I'll take you back to the hotel at the end of the hour." I also promised that I would not call the police or anyone else, and he could still take his life, if he chose to do so. Did I ever pray!

Well, in all the years I have been a member of CBMC, I'm not sure that such a thing has ever occurred before: The speaker didn't show up. When it became apparent that he would not arrive, someone on our committee's executive board asked me if I would speak. I told him that I could not because I had a guest. Finally, they chose another speaker from among those who were in attendance. It could not have been a better choice. The man who spoke also had suffered from a messed-up life, with multiple marriages, and had failed his children in a way strikingly similar to Ed's. The stories could not have tied together better if we had rigged it. But we didn't rig it—God did!

As the speaker related his own story, I could tell that it was having an impact upon Ed. At the end of the meeting, everyone got up to leave, but Ed stayed in his seat—and I stayed right with him. After talking briefly with a few men, the speaker also started to leave. As he walked by our table, Ed grabbed him by the arm and said that he would like to talk with him. Slowly, he asked the speaker to repeat portions of his testimony. Finally, right there in the restaurant, Ed bowed his

head, and using the prayer that the speaker had suggested, he gave his heart to Jesus Christ.

Almost immediately, my new friend contacted both
his first wife and his second wife to tell them that he
had experienced a change in his life. He told his second
wife that he would be returning to California the
following day.

It was only after those calls that I discovered how I
had even become involved in the first place. I learned
that early that morning, Ed had called his present wife
and his ex-wife, to tell them good-bye and to inform
them of his plans to take his life. The first wife, who
lived sixty miles from Chattanooga, quickly telephoned
a friend in Chattanooga. That friend, in turn, had called
me only minutes before he was scheduled to speak at a
meeting. God truly works in mysterious ways!

I had the joy of visiting in Ed's home on the West
Coast on several occasions. In the years following that
first CBMC luncheon he attended, he became a disciple
of Christ and a faithful witness for Him. Several years
later, I received a phone call from Ed's wife telling me
that he was with the Lord. He had gotten up in the mid-
dle of the night, had stumbled over his slippers and lost
his balance. He fell partially through a window and his
throat had been cut. His wife, a registered nurse, told
me that he was dead in ninety seconds.

Perhaps the most amazing thing about this whole
story is that I also learned that Ed's son by his first mar-
riage was a Christian. Through the grace and mercy of
God, Ed got his wish after all—to be able to see his son,
face-to-face, and to tell him, "I'm sorry."

There is no trick or secret to sharing your Christian
faith. It is simply making yourself available and being
usable. Obviously, there was no way that I could have
arranged the circumstances that worked together in
getting Ed to that CBMC luncheon. Only God could
have done that. The timing, for me, had not been good.

I had had a number of pressing business items to attend to. Still, I know that the Lord is vitally interested in every aspect of my life—including my business. Therefore, I can be assured that if I "Seek first His kingdom, and His righteousness," then "all these things [all that I need] shall be added" (Matthew 6:33).

CHAPTER EIGHT

REACHING MEN IS A TEAM EFFORT

No man is an island. John Donne

Two are better than one because they have a good return for their labor. . . . A cord of three strands is not quickly torn apart. Ecclesiastes 4:9–12

I began flying airplanes forty years ago. For most of that period, I have averaged more than 100,000 miles a year in traveling from one place to another, coast to coast. I no longer get a great thrill from flying—after more than 7,000 hours in the air, climbing into a plane is as routine for me as it may be for you to get into an automobile. Yet through the years, the Lord has taught me some great lessons in the air.

Some years ago, I had an experience that has never happened to me before or since. It was a very bad night for flying as I returned from some meetings in Florida. It was raining heavily as I left the airport in south Florida, and the weather briefer told me that conditions in Chattanooga were forecast to go to "zero-zero," meaning there would be no visibility and the clouds would be on the ground by 10:00 P.M.

I proceeded to head north. Shortly after 10:00 that night, my instruments told me that I was just north of Atlanta, Georgia. Since it was still raining and weather conditions had not improved, I decided I had better check to see if the airport in Chattanooga was still open. Ceilings were low in Atlanta, but I could still land if necessary. I requested, and received, permission to leave my assigned radio frequency briefly while I checked the weather in Chattanooga.

As I changed frequencies to check on the Chattanooga weather, I chanced to hear the following: "Does anybody hear me? Does anybody hear me? I need help! Does anybody hear me?"

As any pilot would, I quickly responded, "I hear you. Who are you?" He gave me his airplane number. I asked, "What's the problem?"

He replied, "I'm lost. I need help." I asked the pilot where he was located. He said he did not know for certain. He told me that he was trying to reach Chattanooga.

"How high above the ground are you?" I asked.

"I just flew through some treetops," he answered. "My propeller hit some trees. My altimeter shows that I am 800 feet above the ground."

Any experienced pilot knows that you cannot get to Chattanooga at 800 feet above the ground; there is no path into Chattanooga that low. All this pilot knew was that he was somewhere north of Atlanta. During this time, I asked, and received, permission to change to an emergency frequency to communicate with him. My conversation was being monitored from the ground. The pilot told me that he did not have an instrument rating (to fly on instruments), but he thought that he would be able to keep the wings level. Air traffic control gave him permission to climb to 4,000 feet, which is the minimum altitude to fly into Chattanooga from any direction, to clear the mountains that surround the city.

As the pilot took his plane up to 4,000 feet, he was identified on radar, and ground controllers gave him vectors to fly into Chattanooga. At that moment, the plane had been mere minutes from slamming into the side of a 5,000-foot mountain! He was able to get down onto the ground safely, as was I. I did not meet the pilot, and to this day I do not know who he was.

This incident started me thinking. The Federal Aviation Administration reports that if more pilots would do as that man did—simply cry out for help—many of the people who die in small aircraft crashes could be saved. Unfortunately, many people—whether lost in the air or in a spiritual sense—really don't know they're lost. They don't realize they are in trouble or need help. It also occurred to me that one reason I never hear such cries for help may be because I rarely have occasion to change from the assigned frequencies that are handling instrument-rated pilots. In other words, rather than listening for people who may be in trouble, I'm almost always listening to people who aren't in trouble.

In the air, that is as it should be. I depend upon the radar controller to monitor my flight and to make sure that I am staying on course to reach my destination safely. Therefore, I stay on my assigned radio frequency. In a spiritual sense, however, this may be a reason why many of us fail to hear the voices of those around us who are crying out for help. Quite simply, we are listening on the wrong frequency. We get to a point where we are content to spend our time in "holy huddles"; we don't realize where people around us are spiritually, or what they are doing; we never carefully tune people in. We're not listening. Scores of people we encounter every day are speeding toward physical—and spiritual—death. Many of them are screaming for help, but we are tuned into the wrong frequencies!

I found another lesson in this experience. Although I was the first to make contact with this pilot, I could not help him alone. In a very real sense, it was a classic illustration of teamwork, as the men on the ground helped to guide him in safely after he had been located on radar. There was no way that I could have guided that man to a safe landing. In fact, after he landed, I needed their help myself for sequencing into Chattanooga.

In the previous chapters, I have told you about some of the people that I have met through the years. The Lord has given me the privilege of taking part in the spiritual adventures of many men and women. Yet I hope that one key concept has been clear to you as you have read these stories: It takes teamwork to reach businessmen for Christ!

As a student at Renssalaer Polytechnic Institute, I played on the basketball team. We played against some high-caliber competition. (In fact, my only claim to fame is that I once played against the legendary Bob Cousy in the Boston Garden when he was at Holy Cross.) After I became involved with CBMC, I discovered that the lessons in teamwork which I had learned as a basketball player were equally applicable in my ministry to the businessman.

In CBMC, we work in small, local committees which generally range in size from ten to thirty men. Members of these committee "teams" work together, sharing their gifts, talents, and resources to reach out to the business community around them. These committees are then linked by regional and national CBMC networks which seek to make their individual, personal ministries more effective.

The Scriptures strongly support this team approach to ministry. Proverbs 27:17 tells us that "iron sharpens iron, so one man sharpens another." During His three-year public ministry, the Lord Jesus worked closely with a "team" of twelve men. When He sent them out on their first missionary journey, they went in pairs. After his conversion, the Apostle Paul teamed with Barnabas to begin his own ministry; later he worked closely with Silas, Timothy, and other men. There is limited opportunity for a "Lone Ranger" in today's work of evangelism and discipleship.

This concept of teamwork in CBMC, both locally and nationally, has proved invaluable, particularly in allowing us to follow up on people in various parts of the country and the world. Many years ago, I was introduced to a very successful businessman while I was in Montreal, Canada. The man, a native of New England, was in Canada on business. A mutual friend brought him to a hotel where I was staying so that I might share Jesus Christ with him. The businessman listened with interest, but did not make a decision for the Lord.

However, six months later this man came to Chattanooga on business. He called me when he arrived, and we insisted that he stay in our home. Before he left for home two days later, he had given his heart to Christ. Joyfully, the story does not end there. A year later, the businessman called me from Miami, Florida. He had just arrived there from a business trip to South America.

On the flight back to the States, he was seated next to a very frustrated unsaved businessman. For several hours he had the opportunity to share with the man how Jesus Christ had come into his life and the change the Lord had brought about, not only in his own life, but also in the lives of his wife and five children. The fellow passenger, an attorney, listened with great interest, but did not make a decision to pray to receive Christ. My businessman friend said he had called me simply because he wanted someone to follow up on this lawyer. The man lived in one of the large cities in the north central part of the United States, and we did have an active CBMC in his area. Not only that, but I discovered that a CBMCer lived on the same street as the attorney, only two or three blocks away!

The same night that the businessman called me from Miami, I called the CBMCer in the attorney's hometown to ask him to follow up. The next evening the CBMC member visited the lawyer in his home, continuing to share the gospel message with him. The attorney was astounded. He wondered what kind of secret network we must maintain, in which he would meet another man with the same outlook on life as the man he had been sitting next to on a flight from South America only the day before!

More recently, I was in Washington, D.C., attending a national meeting. The morning after the final session, I went down to the restaurant in the hotel in which my wife and I were staying. Edith said she was going to skip breakfast. There was a long line of people waiting for tables, but there were two seats available at the counter. I chose the one closest to me. Seated next to me was a woman sipping coffee, eating a breakfast roll, and puzzling over a map of the city. Looking over at me, she said, "Mister, do you know anything about Washington?" I told her that I knew a little bit about the city. "Do you know where the Kennedy Center is?" I said yes, and she asked me to show her where it was on the map. Briefly, we discussed how she could get there from the hotel.

"Are you a businessman?" she asked. I told her that I was. "Are you here on a convention?"

I replied, "Well, of sorts." Then she asked me if I knew that Pat Boone and some other prominent entertainers had been on the program for a banquet in the hotel the night before.

"Yes," I said.

"Were you in that meeting?"

"Yes."

She said, "I tried to get in, but I couldn't get a ticket." I told her that I was involved in the meeting. "What was it?" she inquired.

"This is the Year of the Bible," I responded.

"Oh?" she commented.

"Do you know anything about the Bible?" I asked her.

"Not much" was her reply. She added, "If I told you my life story, you wouldn't believe it."

She then proceeded to tell me that she was from Santa Barbara, California, and had traveled to New York City with a lady friend to spend two weeks sightseeing. "I had looked forward to it for a long time," she said, "but things were terrible. My friend didn't like the hotel, didn't like the food, didn't like the waiters, didn't like me, or the room we got. She complained about everything. Last night I lied to her, and said that I had received an emergency phone call and had to leave the city. I did have to leave, or I would have gone crazy. I got on a plane and flew here, even though I didn't have reservations. I don't belong here. Sometimes I think I don't belong anywhere."

I had simply gone into the restaurant to eat breakfast, and this total stranger was telling me her life story! The woman continued to tell me that her husband had walked out on her and their six children, running off with someone else, and had never helped her financially. She said that last year she had married again, but her second husband had lived only a few months and died unexpectedly. She shared a number of other personal things with me and then said, "I don't know why I'm telling you all this. I guess you think I'm crazy. You don't know how I had looked forward to this time—coming back East, seeing some plays, and having a nice time. Everything seems to go wrong."

I'm not very good at talking to women, unless Edith is sitting next to me—and then I usually let her do the talking. But I shared with this woman briefly what Christ had done in my life. "Well, I went to one of those religious meetings one time," she said, "but people were passing out and screaming. I couldn't understand what they were saying. I went a couple of times, but it was so spooky that I never went back. That was years ago."

Then I asked her, "Where did you say you were from?"

"Santa Barbara," she answered.

I inquired if she knew a couple of friends of mine in that city. She didn't know them personally, but she knew the name of the businessman, a prominent real estate developer there.

"Why would you ask if I know them?" she inquired.

"Do you want help?" I asked.

"I've got to have help," she said without hesitation. "I don't need money. I just need help."

I told the woman that if she would give me her name and address, when she returned home next week, I would have the businessman's wife contact her.

It was great to know that at that moment I could say with assurance my friend's wife would call this troubled woman. "What makes you so sure that she'll call me?" the woman asked.

I responded, "Because I know this is what she is giving her life to—people." I could also have said, "And I know that she's on the right frequency."

The woman handed me her business card and said, "I'd be indebted if she would call me."

Then we said good-bye, going our separate ways, and I called the businessman's wife in Santa Barbara. As I knew she would, she contacted the woman soon afterward. I returned to Chattanooga, and did not know what had transpired in that California city until eight weeks later. I had a chance to visit with the Santa Barbara businessman and his wife while we were attending a national CBMC convention in Miami. I learned that during the eight weeks prior to the convention, the two women had met seven times, exploring together the Word of God! During that brief time, the woman's life had already begun to change dramatically.

As I have said before, I am not so much committed to an organization, as to a ministry. But isn't it great to be a part of an organization with people all over the United

States that you can count on! In CBMC, we have many men (and their wives) who are eager and "ready always to give an answer."

In business, we talk in terms of "management teams." In sports, the champion usually is the squad that truly "works together as a team" rather than as a collection of individuals. The same is true, with results that endure for eternity, in evangelism and discipleship. To endeavor to serve the Lord in isolation would be, first of all, very lonely. But even more important, it is impossible. There are too many souls to be won, too many people to be trained "in the nurture and admonition of the Lord."

One other man comes vividly to mind when I consider this vital area of teamwork. This fellow was a bearded hulk of a man, weighing more than 230 pounds. He was an ex-Marine Corps officer who had served on the front lines in Vietnam. In college, he had been a star lineman. After leaving the military, he had found an immediate affinity for working as a stock broker for a large midwestern brokerage firm.

Despite his success in business and in finding a woman he truly loved, this man faced struggles deep within. One day he called upon a prospective client in a neighboring city. The person he called on was a CBMCer, a man who clearly understood that he could not give his life only to building a profitable manufacturing company. His business, in a sense, was his "pulpit" for reaching out to the needy and troubled souls around him. Although I do not suggest that everyone should do this, this particular friend of mine would customarily conclude each conversation, in person or on the telephone, by saying, "God bless you." During his contacts with the midwestern stock broker, this occurred at the end of each visit. The broker, who had quickly developed a fondness and respect for his client, was curious. Not only did the man close each meeting with a sincere "God bless you," but he also exhibited a quality that seemed unusual—and attractive. So when the manufacturer invited the broker to participate in a men's weekend retreat which we hold each year in Wisconsin, the stock broker agreed, primarily out of curiosity.

At the retreat, a series of circumstances occurred which some might label as coincidence; I prefer the term "divine planning." At the registration desk, the broker discovered that he would not be totally among strangers. His father, who had moved to Wisconsin after getting a divorce, was also registered. So was the stock broker's half-brother! The organizers of the retreat had not set up this impromptu reunion, but then I had learned long ago that the Lord is the only true expert in planning. The broker was also startled to discover that each of his three "roommates" for the weekend was affiliated with CBMC: his client was a state CBMC chairman, one of our division directors was there, and I also attended.

At this point, it might be best to let the broker describe in his own words the events that followed:

"The first thing I thought was that I had been assigned to stay with all the generals, and here I was, a rookie. It reminded me of the Bachelor Officers' Quarters in the Marines. When I heard some high-caliber men talking about their relationships with God and Jesus Christ, I was caught off guard. Up until then, my conception of church was that it was something for blue-haired old ladies, mothers with young kids, and an occasional guy who had been roused out of bed to take them to church.

"Some of the guys even had tears in their eyes. In the society I was used to operating in, I had learned that a man doesn't express his hurt, his inner feelings, or that he loves someone. These men seemed to have a different idea.

"I was really getting into what was happening, really impressed. Then my father got up and spoke about what Jesus Christ meant to him. That really blew me away! Here was my dad, who had been the typical non-church person. The mere fact that he got up and spoke meant a lot more to me than anything he had to say.

"As the weekend went on, I sensed a growing feeling of inner peace. Guys weren't ashamed of what they had to say. They told about how Christ could come into your life and change it, just by admitting that you had broken God's laws, asking forgiveness, and inviting Him in."

During that weekend, it was a joy to see what was happening in this young stock broker's life. It was evident that he had been touched by what he had seen and heard and that the Holy Spirit was working in his heart. On the final day of the retreat, I was the speaker. I asked for all the men who wished to make commitments to Jesus Christ to stand up. Almost before the words were out of my mouth, this young man was on his feet. It seemed appropriate, so I asked him if he would share with us how he had reached his decision. This broker spoke for five or six minutes, briefly tracing his life and his realization of how empty it had been without Christ. He humorously commented later, "I found out that this Holy Spirit guy is the executive vice-president in charge of making you talk."

It was exciting to see the change in this man's life, and how a team of businessmen had been used by God to reach him for Christ. It was equally gratifying to know that as we left the retreat, I could ask another dedicated Christian businessman to follow up on him. The CBMCer I contacted, a president of a prestigious investment firm in the same city, quickly got in touch with the broker; and they began to meet for *Operation Timothy,* discussing what the Bible has to say about life today and in eternity. They met weekly, sharing from their lives as brothers in Jesus Christ for more than a year.

Soon after his decision to give his life to the Lord, the young man married the woman he loved. About one year later, their first child was born. When I received the birth announcement, it was a thrill to realize that this infant had been born into a Christian home, to parents who were rapidly learning how to make Jesus Christ the center of their lives. And just think: It all began because God brought together a group of businessmen who teamed up to communicate the importance of having a personal relationship with Jesus Christ! A young man who had been familiar with the value of teamwork in football and in warfare had been reached by the Lord through another kind of "team."

It occurs to me that about now you might have a question in your mind that I am often asked. You may be wondering, if God calls His people from all walks of life, all ages, and all social categories, why I work almost exclusively with businessmen. To me, the answer is simple: There is nothing more natural than being with and working with your peers. I have absolutely nothing against men who choose to work in rescue missions, jails, with children, or with any other group of people. It has been my observation, however, that business and professional men are most effective with other business and professional men.

On several occasions, I have been invited to speak in jail, in the penitentiaries; I have spoken several dozen times at our local rescue mission. The gospel, I realize, is for everyone. Yet I have to confess that I was hopelessly frustrated in my efforts to communicate what God did for me as I stood before these men. I sensed that every one of them knew that I had never walked where they were walking. At that same rescue mission, I have had the privilege of listening to a man who had been saved, after having been on Skid Row for many years. He was unbelievably effective with those men. He could honestly look them in the eye and tell them, "I have walked where you have walked." His story clearly demonstrated that he knew where these men were, that he had once been there himself, and that God had changed him forever. As a result, many men responded to his closing invitation.

Likewise, when I share Jesus Christ with a business or professional man, whether or not I know him, he is willing to listen to what I have to say because I have established credibility as a businessman. To be honest, the call is so obvious for businessmen who know Jesus Christ to carry the message to businessmen who do not know Him, I sometimes have trouble understanding how a person who is *in Christ* and *in the business world* could not have a desire to reach his peers.

Several years ago, a survey was conducted in Chicago among business and professional people in the Loop. One of the questions asked was "With whom would you most like to discuss spiritual things?" The choices were:

1. A member of your family.
2. A clergyman.
3. Some evangelist or missionary.
4. A fellow businessman.

More than 90 percent of the 750 non-Christians interviewed said that they would prefer to talk to a fellow businessman. (Those businessmen who indicated that they were Christians were not tabulated in the survey.) To me, there could be no greater proof that *there are more people who want to hear the gospel than there are people willing to tell about it*—at least in America's business and professional world.

As witnesses for Jesus Christ, we each are participants in the Lord's Great Commission to bring the gospel to all nations. As a team, it can be done.

Our challenge is to determine in which segment of the vast mission field around us God can use us most effectively. For me, the audience is primarily businessmen.

CHAPTER NINE

GOING TO THE CITIES

If we reach the cities . . . we will reach the nation. If we fail in the cities, they will become a cesspool that will infect the entire country.
Dwight L. Moody

Jesus went through towns and villages, teaching the people and making his way toward Jerusalem. Luke 13:22 *(TEV)*

In a very real sense, we have become a nation of spectators. The average American spends hundreds of hours each year sitting passively, absorbing the action on a television screen. Our professional athletes and entertainers are among the highest paid individuals in the country. Many receive alarmingly high salaries to perform so that we can watch. Year round we crowd into stadiums and arenas by the thousands to sit and watch a handful of men compete in baseball, football, basketball, hockey, and other sports.

It is curious that, in many respects, Christians seem to hold the same attitude toward evangelism and discipleship. We rejoice when we hear the response to an evangelistic crusade conducted by Billy Graham, Luis Palau, or any of a number of other gifted speakers. We inwardly shout with joy when our pastors present clear, moving messages on how to establish a personal relationship with Jesus Christ. We enjoy watching televised programs in which famous evangelists challenge the viewers to give their hearts to Christ. And our eyes fill with tears as we read the thrilling accounts of how men and women have come to Christ and undergone amazing transformations. Yet in each of these cases, we are merely spectators.

Unlike sports, however, the mission of evangelism and discipleship has not been given only to the trained professional. I have examined many of our contemporary versions of the Bible, and not one of them renders Matthew 28:19 as, "Go therefore and *watch someone else making disciples. . . .*" Clearly, the Great Commission is given to every Christian, regardless of social status, income, or education. One of our greatest challenges in evangelism, then, is to get the spectators out of their seats and onto the field, so that they can participate in the main event.

This is a particularly important truth in reaching the millions of business and professional men in America for Christ. If we depend upon the efforts of a few dedicated, but limited, individuals, the job will not get done. It is only through hundreds and thousands of faithful Christian businessmen working in concert that our marketplaces will become saturated with the Good News of Jesus Christ. And we can go assured that as we speak, men will listen—since we ourselves come across, not as paid representatives, but as "satisfied customers."

But where do we start? There are countless communities across the United States, and in each we will find businessmen who are lost spiritually. Dare we attempt a shotgun approach to marketplace evangelism? I don't believe that we can. Although we are vitally concerned about the spiritual condition of every man, we also need wisdom in the use of time and resources that the Lord has given us. After much prayer, and as a result of years of experience, we have determined that CBMC's mandate is clear: "Go to the cities."

Throughout the Bible, we see God's concern for the cities. We read about centers of godlessness and wickedness such as Babel, Sodom, and Nineveh in the Old

Testament. The burden Jesus also had for the cities is seen repeatedly in the Gospels. Matthew 11:20 tells us: "Then He began to reproach the cities in which most of His miracles were done, because they did not repent." Isn't it interesting to see how the Lord concentrated His ministry in these great population centers? Christ's concern could also be very specific. "And when He approached [Jerusalem], He saw the city and wept over it" (Luke 19:41).

From the first time that Jesus sent His disciples out, He instructed them to go to the cities. As we read the accounts of the Apostle Paul's travels, his ministry also focuses on the cities! It is obvious that although we are not to ignore the smaller towns and rural communities, there is a spiritual principle in concentrating upon the cities.

I believe this principle contains three points. First of all, the cities are where we find most of the people. A few years ago we discovered that 61 percent of all the people in the United States live in the 100 largest cities and that 85 percent of the population can be found in the top 200 cities. Christ commanded His disciples, "Follow Me and I will make you fishers of men." Any good fisherman knows you are most successful when you go where the fish are!

Second, the large cities are also the centers of influence. Governmental power is found there, as are the corporate offices. In seeking to reach top business and professional men, we discovered they are usually found in the major cities.

The third point concerns the concept of economy of effort. Since the greatest concentrations of people are to be found in the cities, we can utilize the most effective methods to tap our resources and produce a maximum outreach in a minimal time period. To put it another way, we can accomplish more in a shorter time with a smaller team at less expense.

These facts were strongly impressed upon me in 1973 when two of us spent several weeks in New York City seeking to develop an effective way to follow up on our outreach guests. I had been to that great city before, but as we viewed the massive buildings looming above us, I was positively awestruck. It was overwhelming to realize that literally millions of businessmen work in that one city and most of them are desperately, hopelessly lost in God's sight. If I had ever had any illusions of attempting to carry out God's plan singlehandedly, they would have been dashed at that moment.

Consider the number of men working in New York City alone, and then add to that figure the total of business and professional men in the other United States cities. In the top eighty metropolitan areas, there are approximately one hundred twenty-three million people. We estimate that businessmen comprise 7 percent of that number: 8,654,000. That helps to show the magnitude of our mission. Our task is not a difficult one; it is humanly impossible! However, the Bible tells us that "with men it is impossible, but not with God; for all things are possible with God" (Mark 10:27).

As we left New York City to return home, the challenge was clear. The question was "How do we meet it?" When I reported the outcome of our visit to our national board of directors, we presented a successful follow-up plan which consisted of visiting businessmen in their offices. Yet it was sobering to communicate the immensity of the task we faced in reaching the cities, and we all agreed that we needed a plan.

As we pondered this dilemma, I was reminded of a story about a little boy and his destitute family during the Depression. Day after day, his father and mother struggled to feed their children. One day, the young boy announced that he would provide the food for dinner.

"What are you going to do?" his mother asked.

"My friend and I will go down to the pond and catch some fish. There's a bunch of fish there, and we'll be able to catch plenty!" the boy explained.

Proud of the important responsibility he was taking on, the youngster met his friend and they proceeded to the pond a few miles away. When they arrived, they were getting their fishing gear ready when the friend said, "Hey, there's a snake." Excitedly, the boys quickly chased the snake and killed it.

"They say when you see a snake, there are usually others around," the boy told his friend. So they set aside their fishing poles and began stalking their slithering prey. For hours, they romped around the pond, waging a youthful crusade against serpents. Finally, it began to grow dark, so the boys picked up their fishing poles and headed for home.

When the boy arrived home, his mother beheld his broad grin and empty hands. "Wow!" he exclaimed. "Did we ever have a great time. You should have seen how many snakes we killed!"

"Where are the fish you said you were going to catch for us?" his mother asked.

"Oh, uh, we just got so busy chasing and killing snakes that we forgot all about catching fish," the youngster replied apologetically.

Killing snakes! As we pondered this problem of reaching the cities for Christ, we determined that whatever course we took, we would not spend our time killing snakes. We knew what our mission was, and we were not going to become distracted. Years of prayer, research, and planning followed as we sought the Lord's leading in this area.

In September of 1980, our national board gave us a mandate: Go to the cities as we never had before. The result was the creation of what we have called our "Metro 80/80" program, meaning that we would target the eighty largest cities in the United States for a working, established ministry to the business and professional man during the decade of the 1980s.

As we conducted our preliminary research, we discovered that two primary concerns should be addressed when scheduling any ministry activities: physical location and accessibility. We already knew that, to attract businessmen, an attractive meeting site was necessary. We also realized that, regardless of how nice the setting is, we won't get a lost man to come unless he can get there—and return to work—within a minimal amount of time. To address this need, we adopted the concept of what we call "multiple committees." This simply means that instead of building one large committee in a city with perhaps hundreds of members, we would form smaller committees strategically located in key parts of the business community.

In just a few years, this concept has been implemented very effectively in a number of cities, including Minneapolis/St. Paul, Atlanta, Chicago, Houston, Philadelphia, St. Louis, San Francisco, and Washington, D.C. Years ago, for example, there were only two committees in the Twin Cities: one in downtown Minneapolis, and the other in downtown St. Paul. Each committee would sponsor a monthly outreach meeting, and approximately forty men would hear the claims of Christ through a businessman's testimony every month in those two cities. Today, by using the multiple committee concept, we have nearly twenty committees in the Twin Cities; hence each month about five hundred men have an opportunity to hear and respond to the gospel!

Quick and easy access to an outreach meeting is very important. There are so many obstacles to getting a man to such an event that we certainly do not need to present the added problem of time. We have determined that to attract the average, busy businessman, an outreach function has to be held within ten minutes'

walking distance of where he works. This not only
helps in getting a man to a luncheon, but it also greatly
facilitates the office visitation that follows.

I can recall one time in particular when I called on a
fellow who had attended several of our luncheons. He
was not a Christian, but had enjoyed the meetings. For
the past several months, however, he had not attended.
When I asked him about that, he told me that although
he owned his business, he did not feel it was a good use
of his time to take two and a half hours for lunch—one
hour and fifteen minutes for the luncheon itself, and
another hour and fifteen minutes in travel time back
and forth. The round trip required nearly thirty-five
miles of driving, he said, plus the aggravation of trying
to find a place to park, paying a parking fee, occasionally getting caught in a traffic jam and arriving late, and
other related problems. For him, the luncheon added
up to more trouble than it was worth.

As he talked, I was somewhat amused to consider
that although this man did not know Jesus Christ, he
already had a firm grasp on one aspect of stewardship!

Under this plan for establishing small, localized
committees, it is even possible to have a CBMC
designed to minister exclusively to those who work
within one building. This "high-rise outreach" idea
first was tried—very successfully—in Chicago. In that
city, a committee was started in one of the largest buildings which is "home" for approximately 10,000 people.
A small core of Christian businessmen had begun
meeting, both for Bible study and to determine how
they could share their faith with their associates more
fruitfully. A new Christian Business Men's Committee
developed out of this group, and the men proceeded to
schedule their first outreach luncheon and made plans
for follow-up afterward. Thirty-six men (mostly non-
Christians) attended that first event, and seven
responded to the speaker's message by indicating new

decisions for Jesus Christ. The office visitation program which followed was also very successful—and no one had to leave the building in which he worked.

Chicago provides a good example for the value of such strategically located outreach functions. That city alone has twenty-three buildings with more than one million square feet of office space, each housing thousands of workers. Twenty-seven more buildings include more than 650,000 square feet of floor space. A survey of Chicago also showed that although many people live outside of the downtown area, nearly two-thirds of the business and professional men in Chicago have their offices in the downtown area, the "vertical city."

It is amazing when you consider the impact of an outreach event within a single building. It eliminates the need for driving a car on congested city streets, hiring a cab, or using public transportation. In fact, the only mode of transportation required—both for outreach and for follow-up—is the elevator!

There is also the stewardship consideration of making the most of the availability of a speaker when he comes to town. On a number of occasions, I have flown into a city, stayed three days, and have spoken at three breakfasts, three luncheons, and three dinner meetings before flying out again. Every speaker I know who travels frequently would prefer his time be utilized to the maximum. This is particularly true for the speaker who must rely upon commercial airlines. It is of questionable wisdom to travel several hours each way by air just to speak at one businessmen's luncheon for forty minutes. It is more efficient to have several meetings lined up, thus justifying the speaker's time and expense (regardless of who is paying).

Obviously, our purpose in building ministries which focus upon the cities is not just to schedule meetings. Our vision is to see men's lives changed through Christ by the hundreds and thousands. Once these men give their lives to Jesus Christ and are discipled, they can begin the process of multiplying their own efforts by reaching out and sharing Christ with those around them. It is staggering even to imagine the eternal fruit that will be the result!

Not too long ago, I received an inquiry that probably was sent to all of the Christian organizations in the United States. In the letter, I was asked if CBMC was involved in ministering in any way to "unreached people groups." I did not really know exactly how to respond, yet deep in my heart I recognized that business and professional men in America are one of the largest unreached people groups that you could find anywhere on earth. My visit to New York City years ago, and the trip to St. Louis which followed, left me convinced of that. In a large city, it is easy to get lost, in a physical sense. However, unless we can be effective in communicating the biblical truths to business and professional men who inhabit the cities, it is even more likely that they will remain lost spiritually.

The mission for reaching the American businessman for Christ is immense in itself. But the ministry to the business and professional man does not stop there. Ours is a ministry which literally reaches around the world. For instance, each year more than a dozen overseas representatives of Christian businessmen's organizations visit the United States primarily to come and learn our strategy. We have hosted men from countries such as Taiwan, Korea, Australia, New Zealand, India, Mexico, South Africa, the Netherlands, England, Ireland, and Scotland. In recent years, it has become an annual event to send some of our staff and members to train, challenge, and encourage men in those nations to take a vital part in this great mission for Christ.

Not everyone who meets Jesus Christ through our ministry to the businessman is recycled into CBMC.

Through the years, the Lord has used the Christian Business Men's Committee to reach men, and then has led them into seminaries, to full-time pastorates, to foreign mission fields, and into other Christian organizations, including Child Evangelism Fellowship, Campus Crusade for Christ, Youth For Christ, The Navigators, and Fellowship of Christian Athletes. We are not the church, but we are part of the church—the Body of Christ—and it is our privilege and joy to have a small part in the building up of His Body.

As you think of the dozens of sprawling, densely populated cities across our great land, consider the millions of spectators who sit idly while a small group of "players" participate in the warfare of reaching others for Christ. Howard Hendricks, the noted speaker, author, and Bible teacher, put it this way: "The greatest problem in the world today is the unemployment problem. Ninety-five percent of the men and women who are Christians today are unemployed—for Christ. They are active in their churches, but unemployed (in sharing their faith). The end result is that nothing is happening." I am convinced that we are commanded to follow the example of the Lord Jesus:

"And it came about soon afterwards, that He began going about from one city and village to another, proclaiming and preaching the kingdom of God; and the twelve were with Him" (Luke 8:1).

"Now after this the Lord appointed seventy others, and sent them two and two ahead of Him to every city and place where He Himself was going to come. And He was saying to them, 'The harvest is plentiful, but the laborers are few; therefore beseech the Lord of the harvest to send out laborers into His harvest'" (Luke 10:1, 2).

Dwight L. Moody warned years ago that if we fail to reach the American cities for Christ, they will become an urban cesspool that will spread disease throughout the entire nation. I am firmly convinced that if we can succeed in reaching the business and professional men in our cities for Jesus, we will reach the cities as a whole. That, for the Christian Business Men's Committee, is our commitment throughout the 1980s—and, if the Lord tarries, beyond that.

CHAPTER TEN

WHAT ARE YOU GIVING YOUR LIFE TO?

You only go around once in life . . . grab all the gusto you can get. Television commercial

I press on toward the goal for the prize of the upward call of God in Christ Jesus.
Philippians 3:14

I can truthfully say, without hesitation, that the last thirty-plus years of my life have been full and rewarding. I have learned that there is nothing more exciting or satisfying than to share my personal faith in Jesus Christ with others, and, as the Lord presents the opportunities, to play a small part in the spiritual growth of inquisitive, eager new Christians. Let me explain how I came to the point of deciding exactly how I would use the rest of my life, and some of the events that influenced that decision.

I mentioned earlier that I am one of those people who came to Jesus Christ several years after joining a church. It took that long for me to discover that God does not operate on a 50:50 quota system, with the top half (the "good" people) going to heaven and the lower half (the "bad" guys) going to hell. I had often spent time wondering which half God had me assigned to, until an uncle took me to a meeting—which didn't happen to be in a church—where for the first time I heard a clear-cut definition of what it means to be a Christian. The speaker that night explained that a Christian was simply someone who has had all his sins—past, present, and future—forgiven by God.

I might have heard it somewhere before, but for the first time I understood that sin is the only thing that separates us from God. In the final analysis, the speaker pointed out, this problem of sin has to be dealt with on an individual basis if we are to have a personal relationship with God. He cited 2 Corinthians 5:21, which says that God made Jesus Christ to be sin for us; and because He (Jesus Christ) had no sin of His own, we can have the righteousness of God through Jesus Christ. That night I could not have quoted one verse in the entire Bible. Until that time, I had hardly ever even looked at a Bible. Yet because of what that man had said and because of the ministry of the Holy Spirit in my life, I became a believer in Jesus Christ.

After I had finished repeating the sinner's prayer, the speaker offered the best counsel any new believer can be given. He said that as a Christian, I should read God's Word every day. For some reason, I never questioned that suggestion, and I have been reading the Scriptures on a daily basis now for more than forty years.

This was particularly important to me because I did not have an opportunity to receive good, gospel-centered teaching immediately after my conversion. I am confident that the only thing that kept me from getting into deep sin was the daily feeding I received directly from the Word of God. Even during my time as a Navy pilot during World War II, I was the only member of my squadron who took out the Bible each day and read it. I took a lot of ribbing about it, but perhaps God gave me a thick skin so I could ignore my critics and keep on reading.

I don't say this to sound in any way boastful. It is a simple fact that the best way to get to know someone is to spend time with him. During those important early years of my Christian life, I had the joy of getting to know God by spending time in His Word and talking to Him in prayer.

I learned many things by reading the Bible. To be frank, many of the things I read then I did not understand; some things I still don't understand today. But one thing that literally leaped out at me from the pages of the Scriptures was that I must marry a Christian girl. As far as I know, when I began going out with Edith, she was the first Christian girl I had ever dated. After the war ended, we got married. From the beginning we began reading the Bible and praying together. As the years have passed, I have seen how important it was to become one in our commitment to the Lord. The Lord has blessed us with a ministry, as a couple, that we could never have had as individuals.

I was in my last year of college when we got married. I was attending Renssalaer Polytechnic Institute, and perhaps because I had been in school so long (taking time out for the Navy, and all), I was asked to join the faculty. My assignment was to teach Advanced Cost Accounting, and I had the privilege of teaching under the professor who was perhaps the most beloved on the campus. This man was an excellent educator; he was good looking and young, in his late thirties. He had inherited some money from a relative, and that had enabled him to drive the biggest Lincoln available and to buy the loveliest home of any of the teachers I knew. To sum it up, he became my ideal. I concluded that it would be great to be rich, intelligent, popular, and to know as much about as many subjects as he did.

One winter evening we stayed up to nearly midnight, grading papers in his office. Afterward, we began trudging in the deep snow of upstate New York toward our respective homes. Shortly before we parted company at his house, he said something to me that stunned me: "Ted, I've come to the conclusion that nothing in life makes any sense." I didn't quite know how to respond to that statement, so I feebly inquired if he had ever tried "religion." My revered professor replied that he had studied all of the major religions of the world on site, spending his summers traveling all over the world to find out what people believed and why they believed it. I asked him if he had ever considered Christianity, and he commented that he had looked at that, too.

I was taken back by this brief conversation. Here was a man who, in my mind, had it all. Yet he had just stated quite plainly that "nothing in life makes any sense."

The following June I graduated, but that talk remained fresh in my mind. The next fall, on the opening day of school, an event occurred which would imprint itself forever in my mind. My friend, the professor, took his life.

I will never forget looking at his body in the casket and thinking: *Some preacher is going to have to pay for not getting the gospel to this man.* Ironically, I had been with him on literally hundreds of occasions, yet it had never occurred to me that I had any responsibility for sharing my own faith with him. I left the funeral home devastated. The man who had had everything now had nothing. I was very troubled that someone had not introduced him to Jesus Christ, but at that time I failed to realize the role I could have played.

Meanwhile, my working career was getting off to a good start. Upon graduation, I took my first job in a management training program with the Arrow Shirt Company, in its largest plant, which was located in Troy, New York. Just a few months before the end of the training program, I, at age twenty-three, was given the responsibility for all shirt manufacturing. This meant that I oversaw the work of 550 people, and I had a full management team reporting to me. At that time, the plant was producing 10,000 dozen shirts a week. Daily, I dealt with people ranging from engineers and quality control people to foremen, machinists, and sewing machine operators. I also was involved in negotiations with the local union. It was a challenging job, truly a "plum" for a new college graduate.

I had no complaints about the job, yet after I had been in this position for nearly two years, I typed a letter of resignation and took it to the front office. I hadn't even mentioned anything about it to my wife. When the plant manager read the letter, he was shocked. He asked me why I wanted to leave.

I told him, "Frankly, I'm not sure why I'm leaving. All I know is that I can't give my life to making shirts." The manager asked me what I planned to do. I admitted that I didn't have the faintest idea, except that I was convinced that I was a round peg in a square hole, or perhaps a square peg in a round hole. I just knew that I couldn't go on.

That was not a good enough reason for the plant manager. He took my letter and tore it into pieces, throwing it into his wastebasket. He suggested that I take a few days off; there was no way that the company would consider accepting my resignation. I was perplexed. I was almost twenty-five years old and had a job any college graduate two years out of school would have loved to have. Yet I was unhappy. Even worse, the company wouldn't let me quit.

I continued working for three more months, not knowing how to get out of the job. Finally, I went back to the plant manager's office a second time. I told him that I wasn't going to write any more letters of resignation, but I would be leaving on March 1. I went on to say that after that date, I would never set foot in the plant again. I really wasn't mad at anyone, but I wanted to impress upon him that I was sincere. He tried to talk me out of it, offering a raise in pay or suggesting I be transferred to manage one of the other plants. I simply

told him that I was not interested and would not consider any alternatives.

When I told Edith I had quit, she could hardly believe
it. She asked me what I was going to do. I told her I
didn't know, except that I could not give my life to making shirts. It wasn't as if we were financially secure for
an indefinite time; after my resignation became
effective, we were left with exactly $800 in the bank. I
had no immediate prospects for additional income, and
we faced payments on two cars and rent due each
month. We also had to provide for the first of our three
daughters, who was by this time nearly a year old. I'm
sure Edith thought that she had married a nut!

During the next several weeks I interviewed for jobs
in Saudi Arabia, Aruba, Trinidad, Lancaster, Pennsyl-
vania, and other places. However, none of the job offers
I received sparked my interest. What a predicament: no
income, no job, and no ideas about what I wanted to do.

At this time my cousin, Art DeMoss, came to the rescue. Art had become a Christian just a few months
earlier. He was in the life and health insurance business; hearing that I was unemployed, he came by our
home one evening. He asked if I would consider selling
insurance. As I think back to my response at the time, I
have to laugh. I told him I would never do that if it were
the last job on the face of the earth. Then I proceeded to
inform him that I regarded insurance salesmen as
"peddlers" and assured him that I could not give my life
to doing that, any more than I could dedicate myself to
shirt manufacturing.

Despite my bold replies, I was talking from a position
of weakness. Our small money reserve was running
out, and I needed to do something to pay our bills.
Finally, I told Art I would try to sell insurance for a
while, just to earn some money, and that I would leave
as soon as I found a job I liked. Fortunately, my cousin
accepted those conditions.

I faced an immediate obstacle, since I did not have a license to sell insurance and it would take time to study for the New York State licensing exam. In the meantime, I went out with one of Art's better salesmen for a few days to observe firsthand how a person sells insurance—I couldn't have had more fun if I had been with Bob Hope. This man had a wonderful sense of humor, truly seemed to enjoy people, and was making a lot of money without (it seemed) doing a lot of work. It was a great introduction to the insurance business for me, and helped to dispel my misconceptions about the industry.

After I received my license, I discovered that I could earn as much money selling insurance in one week (the very first week, in fact) as I had been earning in a full month at the shirt company. Soon I was doing very well financially, but after several months I sensed that I was again "trapped," this time by golden handcuffs. Instead of making shirts, I was selling insurance; and I was convinced that I could not give my life to doing either. Again I wanted to quit my job, but I couldn't think of anything else I wanted to do.

What I found most disconcerting was the thought that perhaps I would never find anything that would satisfy me. It never occurred to me that I should pray about my dilemma, but I could not help but wonder what God wanted me to do with my life.

At this point, Art invited me to my first CBMC prayer meeting in Albany. As I watched this group praying faithfully for dozens of unsaved men by name, I became challenged. My eyes began to be opened—slowly, but through God's grace they did open. For instance, the first time they talked to me about reaching people for Christ, I responded with a statement that this was "not our job." Our job, I told them, was to make money and put it into the offering plate, so that the preachers could win the lost to Christ. I could not have been further from the truth, but that shows you the level of my thinking at that point.

Later when I had the joy of introducing the eighty-one-year-old man to Christ, I learned a lot more than just the understanding that it does not require a seminary education to effectively witness for the Lord. For the first time, I gained a new perspective on my life's work. That incident showed me that as a Christian, a businessman should look upon his job as his *avocation.* I learned that my true vocation as a believer is to share the good news of Jesus Christ with others. Suddenly, my dilemma was resolved. I realized that there was no way that a job in itself could satisfy a believer, regardless of how much money it paid, how much success it could offer, or how much worldly acclaim it could provide.

In Mark 13:31, Jesus says, "Heaven and earth will pass away, but My words will not pass away." I am fully convinced that unless we give our lives to the two things that last forever—the Word of God and people—Christians will continually find their lives to be frustrating and empty.

Some time ago, I met a man who said that his goal, before becoming a Christian, was to become the richest man in the cemetery! He had thought that it would really be something if people would walk by his tombstone, point to it, and say, "There lies the richest man in the whole cemetery." Such a goal seems ridiculous to us, but for years that had been his driving purpose in life.

As you would expect, that all changed when he came to know Jesus Christ. For many years now, this fellow has found that a new focus for his life has brought greater fulfillment than he ever could have imagined. Today he is giving his life to people. Specifically, he is involved in winning and discipling men and their families to Jesus Christ. In fact, the magnitude of this commitment is startling. One time I spoke at a dinner party he sponsored personally, and more than forty of his guests indicated that they had prayed to accept Christ for the first time. Within three weeks, he had thirty of them in Bible study, seeking to introduce them to the Word of God so that they could better understand their position in Christ. Some of those who agreed to begin the Bible study weren't even Christians, despite the indication that they had prayed to receive Christ at the close of the meeting. But at least they were spiritually open, which made it even more important to get them promptly into God's Word.

On another occasion I spoke to a gathering of some of this man's unsaved friends. Within the next few days he contacted sixteen of those who had attended. He arranged to meet at breakfast, lunch, or dinner with each one of them personally. He would have breakfast with one man on Monday morning, another man Monday noon, and a third Monday evening. So it continued throughout the week. On each occasion, his sole purpose was to invite his guest to join him in an introductory study of the Word of God. He was confident that this exposure would give him a desire for the sincere milk of the Word, help him to begin growing in the Lord, and mold him into a useful vessel. This man, obviously, has come a long way from the cemetery!

At this point, I have an obvious question that I would like to address to you. To what are *you* giving your life? Dr. James Dobson, the noted Christian psychologist, has summed up this situation well.

Jim said, "I have concluded that the accumulation of wealth, even if I could achieve it, is an insufficient reason for living. When I reach the end of my days, a moment or two from now, I must look back on something more meaningful than the pursuit of houses and lands and machines and stocks and bonds. Nor is fame of any lasting benefit. I will consider my earthly existence as to have been wasted unless I can recall a loving family, a consistent investment in the lives of people, and an earnest attempt to serve the God who made me. Nothing else makes much sense."

I could not say it any better. As I reflect upon this life, it seems to me that, to a point, my professor friend's evaluation of life was correct. Sadly, he had not gone far enough. Without God, and ultimately without realizing that we are living witnesses for Jesus Christ, life does not seem to make much sense. Happily, with Christ our lives take on infinite meaning and importance.

I'm extremely grateful for that small handful of men in upstate New York who challenged me about the second greatest mission in life: to make Jesus Christ known in the marketplace where I live, work, and play. Nothing else could approach being the second best thing in life—with knowing Christ personally as the *best* thing in life.

I want to challenge you to rethink your goals, your priorities. To what are you giving your life? Is it wood, hay, or stubble? Or is it the mission that we all share— that of being ambassadors for the Lord Jesus every day we live? If you are unsure about how you want to invest the remainder of your life, I encourage you to pray about it. Ask the Lord if He would not want you to make yourself available to Him. You may find the return on your investment far beyond your dreams!

You may contact the
Christian Business Men's Committee
by writing

CBMC
1800 McCallie Ave.
Chattanooga, TN 37404

The following materials have been developed by
the Christian Business Men's Committee for use in
evangelism and discipleship. They are available
from CBMC of USA and may be ordered on this form.

Quantity	Price
The Reason Why	.75
Steps To Peace With God	.10
First Steps - 4 part Bible study	$1.50
How To Follow-Thru	$2.50
Operation Timothy Packet	$6.95

Total _____

Shipping & Handling (Add 10%) _____

Total Enclosed _____

Name_____

Street Address_____

City_____ State_____ Zip _____

Phone (   )_____

Mail order to: Christian Business Men's Committee of USA
                   P.O. Box 3308
                   Chattanooga, Tennessee 37404
                    615/698-4444